Bisquick™

QUICK TO THE TABLE

Betty Crocker

Bisquick™

QUICK TO THE TABLE

Easy Recipes for Food You Want to Eat

Houghton Mifflin Harcourt

Boston • New York • 2020

GENERAL MILLS

Global Business Solutions
Director: Heather Polen

Global Business Solutions
Manager: Andrea Kleinschmit

Executive Editor:
Cathy Swanson Wheaton

Recipe Development and Testing:
Betty Crocker Kitchens

Photography: General Mills
Photography Studios and Tony
Kubat Photography

HOUGHTON MIFFLIN HARCOURT

Editorial Director: Deb Brody

Associate Editor: Sarah Kwak

Senior Managing Editor:
Marina Padakis

Production Editor: Christine Borris

Art Director and Book Design:
Tai Blanche

Senior Production Coordinator:
Kimberly Kiefer

Published by Houghton Mifflin Harcourt Publishing Company

For information about permission to reproduce selections from this book, write to Permissions, Houghton Mifflin Harcourt Publishing Company, 3 Park Avenue, New York, New York 10016.

hmhbooks.com

Library of Congress Cataloging-in-Publication Data

Names: Crocker, Betty, author.
Title: Betty Crocker bisquick quick to the table : easy recipes
   for food you want to eat.
Other titles: Bisquick quick to the table
Description: Boston : Houghton Mifflin Harcourt, 2020. |
   Includes index.
Identifiers: LCCN 2019057819 (print) | LCCN 2019057820
   (ebook) | ISBN 9780358331582 (trade paperback) |
   ISBN 9780358330028 (ebook)
Subjects: LCSH: Cooking, American. | Food mixes. |
   Quick and easy cooking. | Gluten-free diet—Recipes.
Classification: LCC TX715 .C9213834 2020 (print) |
   LCC TX715 (ebook) | DDC 641.5973—dc23
LC record available at https://lccn.loc.gov/2019057819
LC ebook record available at https://lccn.loc.gov/2019057820

Manufactured in the United States of America

DOC 10 9 8 7 6 5 4 3 2 1

Cover photo: Mexican Waffle Bowls (page 101)

Find more great ideas at
BettyCrocker.com

GOOD NEWS!

I know getting meals on the table isn't always easy. You're looking for solutions that are easy to make *and* easy on your budget, as well as being delicious enough to entice your household food critics. That may be a tall order for some—but not for Bisquick! Look inside and see all the fantastic, **exclusive recipes** (you won't find them anywhere else) for the way you eat today.

You'll find pumped-up flavors and lightened-up dishes filled with colorful, yummy ingredients you and your family will love. From **15-minute prep** recipes to those using **8 ingredients or less** (not counting salt, pepper, oil or water) and **ready in 30 minutes**, you'll find a sensational solution no matter what time of day or occasion. Eating gluten-free? You'll love the wide variety of gluten-free recipes here, including the **Basics Smash-Ups**: all our favorite Bisquick recipes written with *both* original and gluten-free instructions, together as one!

Wake 'em up with creative new pancake and waffle recipes, such as **Churro Pancakes** and **Bacon, Corn and Hash Brown Waffles**. Is brunch your jam? Try our new **Chocolate-Coconut French Toast Strata**. Need a partner for chicken? **Twice-Baked Garlic Bread** is the perfect match. Craving a new "wow" appetizer? Try our **Bloody Mary Waffle Bites**. Is dinner on the go tonight? How about **Mini Corn Dog Muffins**? What to serve at your meeting? Bring in some **Gluten-Free Zucchini, Peanut Butter and Chocolate Bars**.

And don't miss these fabulous features:

- **Crazy Night Survival Guide**, for those nights when there's no time and no plan.
- **5 Creative Breakfasts on the Go**, great for when you can't sit down for a proper meal.
- **Baking Breakfast Together**, to turn making breakfast into a fun activity with your kids!
- **Sausage Cheese Ball Appetizers**, a most-requested recipe with yummy twists.
- **Muffin Cup Meals**, using your muffin pans for great family meals on-the-go.
- **Mix-It-Up Mug Treats**, super-fast microwave treats to satisfy your sweet tooth!

With all this great information and helpful recipes, let this book be your meal-time game plan!

Let's pop open your yellow and blue Bisquick box and dig in!

CONTENTS

BISQUICK—YOUR SUPERHERO MEAL SOLUTION

If we could give it a cape, we would. Bisquick in your pantry means you can breathe easy. It's the start of incredible dishes for any meal, any occasion. You get hot, homemade food on your table without breaking a sweat, and your family gets to dig in!

Baking with Bisquick

Measure Correctly Spoon it into your dry measuring cup and level with a straight-edge knife or spatula. To avoid overmeasuring, don't scoop the Bisquick mix into the cup; pack it in or tap the cup.

Keep It Fresh Store it in an airtight container or plastic bag in a cool, dry place, such as your pantry shelf. If you want to keep it longer or if you live in a warm, humid area, you can store it in your refrigerator or freezer; just bring it to room temperature before using it.

Sticky Situation Bisquick will react to fluctuations in humidity, just like any other flour-based product. In humid conditions, you may find batters or doughs are a little stickier, softer or runnier. You can add an additional tablespoon or two of Bisquick to make the dough or batter easier to work with.

No Switching Original Bisquick and Bisquick Gluten Free are very different from each other and therefore shouldn't be used in recipes if they don't specifically call for that type of Bisquick mix. See page 11 for specific information about baking with Bisquick Gluten Free. Check out our Basics Smash-Ups (starting on page 15) for both the Original and Gluten Free versions of each recipe. We also have a variety of recipes that call for Bisquick Gluten Free throughout this book that are so good even those who can eat gluten won't miss it!

Great Pancakes and Waffles

WAFFLE SIZES

There are many different types of waffle makers! Two-square and 4-square or round, Belgian and regular waffle makers can be found when searching stores or the internet. Most of our recipes (unless otherwise noted) were tested in one of the most common waffle makers—a round, 6½-inch regular waffle maker.

The amount of batter needed to fill your waffle iron, typically ¼ cup to ½ cup, will depend not only on the size and shape of your waffle maker but on the thickness of the batter. This will also affect your pancake yield, so use the recipe yields as a general guideline. You can bake a test waffle to get the perfect amount of batter figured out.

No Griddle? If you don't own a pancake griddle, you can use any 8- to 12-inch skillet you have. If the recipe you are using calls for a nonstick griddle or pan, be sure to use one, if possible, for the best results.

Avoid Buildup If your griddle or waffle iron isn't nonstick or is older, you may need to grease it between each batch. We prefer to use a pastry brush to lightly brush vegetable oil on the griddle or waffle iron rather than using cooking spray, as it can create a residue on both the griddle or waffle iron surface and sides (from the overspray). This requires additional cleanup to keep the waffle iron looking nice and performing well. If a recipe has specific instructions for greasing, follow those for the best success.

Wait for the Sizzle Griddles are hot enough when you wet your fingers lightly, flick the water from them onto the griddle and it sizzles. You can also make a test pancake to be sure the heat is at the right level to cook the pancakes correctly.

PANCAKE AND WAFFLE QUICK FIXES

Pancake or Waffle Problem	Quick Fix
Raw in the center	Too little liquid, too much Bisquick mix, causing batter to be too thick, or griddle/waffle iron temperature is too high
Leathery or tough	Dry, leathery: Griddle/waffle iron temperature is too low Tough: Griddle/waffle iron temperature is too high
Dark outsides	Griddle/waffle iron temperature is too high
Too crispy	Overgreased waffle iron, too much liquid or not enough Bisquick mix

THICK AND FLUFFY PANCAKES

If you're a fan of thick and fluffy pancakes, simply add an additional tablespoon or two of Bisquick to the batter. This is another great time to try a test pancake. You may wish to reduce the temperature of your griddle slightly so the pancake inside has a chance to cook before the outside gets too brown. Keep in mind that the batter will continue to thicken the longer it stands.

STORING PANCAKES OR WAFFLES

Make a big batch and freeze them, and breakfast will be effortless on your busy days. But don't box them into just breakfast—keep them on standby for other quick meals! (See page 28 for throw-together dinner ideas.)

1. Cool pancakes or waffles completely in a single layer on a cooling rack.
2. Store in an airtight container or resealable food-storage plastic bag in the refrigerator for up to 2 days or in the freezer for up to 3 months.

HOW TO REHEAT PANCAKES OR WAFFLES

1 pancake or waffle	Uncovered on microwavable plate on High 20 to 30 seconds
3 pancakes	Uncovered on microwavable plate on High 1 minute
Waffles	Toast in toaster until warm inside and desired color on outside

Baking Gluten-Free

Whether you have a gluten sensitivity or you just choose to avoid it, here's the skinny on how to bake gluten-free. Gluten is a protein that naturally occurs in certain grains like wheat, barley, rye and some oats. Foods that are naturally gluten-free can contain gluten if they have been processed in a plant where gluten foods are made or made in a kitchen with utensils that have been used with foods containing gluten.

In order to bake gluten-free, you need to replace all-purpose flour (which is made with wheat and therefore has gluten) with a variety of other flours that can act as a substitute, including white rice, brown rice, tapioca, sorghum and potato starch. Or you can use Bisquick Gluten Free!

It's important to use recipes specifically developed for Bisquick Gluten Free (we've included many in this book) to get successful baked goods that are delicious to eat. You can't substitute regular Bisquick for Gluten Free or vice versa. Here in the Betty Crocker Kitchens, we work hard to make gluten-free recipes as close as possible to recipes made with all-purpose flour, so you won't feel like you're missing a thing! During taste panels, we were so excited to find out what we were tasting and seeing was a gluten-free recipe—we never would have guessed it!

Tips and Tricks

TO BE GLUTEN-FREE OR NOT TO BE

These products may or may not contain gluten. Many products will say "gluten-free" somewhere on the label, but these may not. If you're unsure if it's gluten-free, call the manufacturer.

Artificial extracts (almond, vanilla, etc.)	Barbecue sauces and marinades
Bouillon cubes or granules	Broths or gravies
Candy	Coating mixes
Flavorings	Imitation bacon
Meat substitutes	Miso
Processed meats	Rotisserie chicken
Salad dressings	Sauces
Soups	Soy sauce

Keep It Separate For those who are gluten-sensitive, it matters. It's necessary to keep a dedicated space for storing ingredients when cooking gluten-free as well as keeping separate cutting boards and utensils such as rubber scrapers and metal spatulas. It's hard to completely remove any gluten residue from these kitchen items, and gluten-free foods can easily become contaminated by even the tiniest bit of residue left on a utensil or countertop.

Pan Prep Grease pans with solid shortening or spray with cooking spray without flour.

Spoon It Use the same measuring method as for Original Bisquick (page 8).

Liquid Absorption Gluten-free doughs may absorb liquids differently than wheat dough, so follow directions carefully.

Dough Handling Gluten-free doughs tend to be sticky. Wet or grease hands to prevent the dough from sticking.

Is It Done Yet? Gluten-free baked goods often look done before they actually are, so follow the doneness directions given in addition to bake time.

"I'm amazed at what a great product Bisquick Gluten Free is. It doesn't have the off flavors and gritty texture I see in many other gluten-free products."

—Nancy, Bisquick recipe developer, gluten-free since 2010

Always read labels to make sure each recipe ingredient is gluten-free. Products and ingredient sources can change.

13

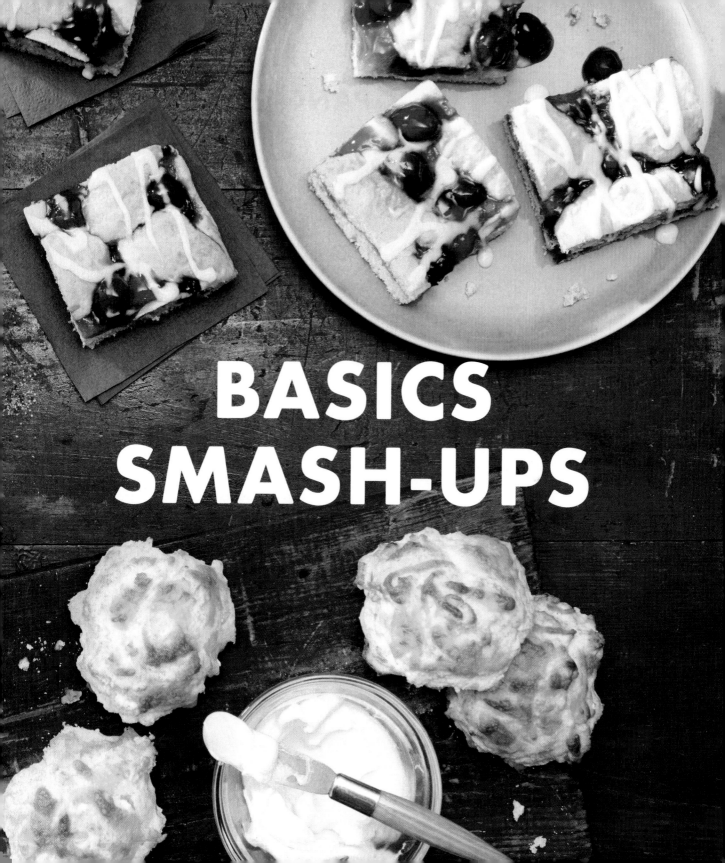

BASICS
SMASH-UPS

CLASSIC PANCAKES

ORIGINAL: PREP TIME: 20 minutes | START TO FINISH: 20 minutes

GLUTEN FREE: PREP TIME: 20 minutes | START TO FINISH: 20 minutes

INGREDIENTS	ORIGINAL	GLUTEN FREE
	Makes 14 pancakes	Makes 10 pancakes
Original Bisquick mix	2 cups	
Bisquick Gluten Free mix		1 cup
Milk	1 cup	1 cup
Vegetable oil		2 tablespoons
Eggs	2	1
Toppings (if desired)	Butter, maple-flavored syrup	Butter, gluten-free maple-flavored syrup

1 Heat griddle or skillet over medium-high heat (375°F). Brush griddle with vegetable oil if necessary.

2 In medium bowl, stir all ingredients except toppings until blended.

3 For each pancake, pour slightly less than ¼ cup batter onto hot griddle. Cook about 2 minutes or until bubbles form on top and edges are dry. Turn; cook until golden brown.

4 Serve with toppings.

Save Time: Place cooked pancakes on cooling rack until completely cooled. Transfer to zipper-top freezer bag. To reheat, place 3 pancakes on microwavable dinner plate. Microwave on High about 1 minute or until hot.

Gluten Free Pancake

CLASSIC WAFFLES

	ORIGINAL	GLUTEN FREE
ORIGINAL: PREP TIME: 20 minutes	START TO FINISH: 20 minutes	
GLUTEN FREE: PREP TIME: 20 minutes	START TO FINISH: 20 minutes	

INGREDIENTS	ORIGINAL Makes 6 (6½-inch) waffles	GLUTEN FREE Makes 8 (6½-inch) waffles
Original Bisquick mix	2 cups	
Bisquick Gluten Free mix		1⅓ cups
Milk	1⅓ cups	1¼ cups
Vegetable oil	2 tablespoons	3 tablespoons
Eggs	1	1
Toppings (if desired)	Butter, syrup	Butter, gluten-free peach preserves

1 Brush waffle maker with vegetable oil or spray with cooking spray. Heat waffle maker.

2 In medium bowl, stir all waffle ingredients except toppings until blended.

3 Pour about ½ cup batter onto center of hot waffle maker. Close lid of waffle maker. Bake about 5 minutes or until steaming stops. Carefully remove waffle.

4 Serve with desired toppings.

Save Time: Place cooked waffles on cooling rack until completely cooled. Transfer to zipper-top freezer bag. To reheat, toast waffles in toaster until hot.

Gluten Free Classic Waffles

FRUIT SWIRL COFFEE CAKE

ORIGINAL: PREP TIME: 20 minutes | START TO FINISH: 45 minutes

GLUTEN FREE: PREP TIME: 20 minutes | START TO FINISH: 45 minutes

INGREDIENTS	ORIGINAL Makes 18 servings	GLUTEN FREE Makes 18 servings
COFFEE CAKE		
Original Bisquick mix	4 cups	
Bisquick Gluten Free mix		1 box (3 cups)
Granulated sugar	½ cup	⅔ cup
Milk	½ cup	¾ cup
Vanilla	1 teaspoon	2 teaspoons
Almond extract	1 teaspoon	
Eggs	3	4
Butter, melted		½ cup
1 can (21 oz) pie filling (any flavor)	1	1
GLAZE		
Powdered sugar	1 cup	1 cup
Milk	2 tablespoons	2 tablespoons

1 **Original:** Heat oven to 350°F. Spray bottom and sides of 15 × 10 × 1-inch pan with cooking spray. **Gluten Free:** Heat oven to 375°F. Use cooking spray.

2 In large bowl, stir all Coffee Cake ingredients except pie filling; beat vigorously with spoon 30 seconds. Spread two-thirds of the batter (about 2½ cups) in pan. Spread pie filling over batter (filling may not cover batter completely). Drop remaining batter by tablespoons onto pie filling.

3 Bake 20 to 25 minutes or until light brown.

4 Meanwhile, in small bowl, stir Glaze ingredients until smooth and thin enough to drizzle. Drizzle glaze over warm coffee cake. Serve warm or cool.

Gluten Free Fruit Swirl Coffee Cake

Gluten Free Easy Cheese Drop Danish

EASY CHEESE DROP DANISH

* 15-minute prep
* 30 minutes or less

ORIGINAL: PREP TIME: 10 minutes | START TO FINISH: 25 minutes

GLUTEN FREE: PREP TIME: 15 minutes | START TO FINISH: 25 minutes

	ORIGINAL	GLUTEN FREE
INGREDIENTS	Makes 12 Danish	Makes 12 Danish
CREAM CHEESE FILLING		
Cream cheese, softened	3 ounces	3 ounces
Granulated sugar	1 tablespoon	1 tablespoon
Milk	1 tablespoon	1 tablespoon
DANISH		
Original Bisquick mix	2 cups	
Bisquick Gluten Free mix		1¾ cups
Butter, softened	¼ cup	½ cup
Granulated sugar	2 tablespoons	2 tablespoons
Milk	⅔ cup	⅔ cup
VANILLA GLAZE		
Powdered sugar	¾ cup	¾ cup
Milk	1 tablespoon	1 tablespoon
Vanilla	¼ teaspoon	¼ teaspoon

1 Heat oven to 450°F. Spray cookie sheet with cooking spray. **Gluten Free:** Use cooking spray without flour.

2 In small bowl, mix cream cheese and granulated sugar with spoon until smooth; stir in 1 tablespoon milk. Set aside.

3 In medium bowl, stir Bisquick mix, butter and 2 tablespoons granulated sugar until crumbly. Stir in ⅔ cup milk until dough forms; beat with spoon 15 strokes.

4 On cookie sheet, drop dough by rounded tablespoonfuls about 2 inches apart. Make a shallow well in center of each with back of spoon; fill each with about 1 teaspoon filling.

5 Bake 8 to 10 minutes or until golden brown.

6 Meanwhile, in small bowl, mix Vanilla Glaze ingredients until smooth and drizzling consistency. Drizzle glaze over warm Danish. Store covered in refrigerator.

Fruit-Filled Drop Danish

ORIGINAL: Substitute any flavor preserves for the Cream Cheese Filling.

GLUTEN FREE: Use gluten-free preserves.

Original Banana Nut Bread

BANANA NUT BREAD

15-minute prep
8 ingredients or less

ORIGINAL: PREP TIME: 15 minutes | START TO FINISH: 3 hours 25 minutes

GLUTEN FREE: PREP TIME: 15 minutes | START TO FINISH: 3 hours 25 minutes

INGREDIENTS	ORIGINAL	GLUTEN FREE
	Makes 1 loaf (16 slices)	Makes 1 loaf (16 slices)
Mashed, very ripe bananas	1⅓ cups (2 large)	1⅓ cups (2 large)
Sugar	⅔ cup	⅔ cup
Milk	¼ cup	¼ cup
Vegetable oil	3 tablespoons	¼ cup
Vanilla	½ teaspoon	½ teaspoon
Eggs	3	3
Original Bisquick mix	2⅔ cups	
Bisquick Gluten Free mix		2 cups
Chopped nuts	½ cup	½ cup

1 Heat oven to 350°F. Grease bottom only of 9×5-inch loaf pan or spray with cooking spray. **Gluten Free:** Use cooking spray without flour.

2 In large bowl, mix bananas, sugar, milk, oil, vanilla and eggs. Stir in Bisquick mix and nuts. Pour batter into pan.

3 **Original:** Bake 50 to 60 minutes or until toothpick inserted in center comes out clean. Cool 10 minutes. Run knife or metal spatula around sides of pan to loosen bread; remove from pan to cooling rack. Cool completely, about 2 hours. **Gluten Free:** Bake 55 to 60 minutes.

Kitchen Secret: This bread freezes well and is great to have on hand when company drops in. Freeze by wrapping it tightly in heavy-duty foil for up to 2 months. To store, wrap bread tightly in plastic wrap or foil. Store at room temperature up to 4 days, or refrigerate up to 10 days.

Kitchen Secret: For the best flavor, be sure to use bananas that are very ripe.

- 15-minute prep
- 30 minutes or less

APPLESAUCE SPICE DOUGHNUTS

ORIGINAL: PREP TIME: 10 minutes | START TO FINISH: 20 minutes

GLUTEN FREE: PREP TIME: 10 minutes | START TO FINISH: 20 minutes

	ORIGINAL	GLUTEN FREE
INGREDIENTS	Makes 8 doughnuts and doughnut holes	Makes 10 doughnuts and doughnut holes
DOUGHNUTS		
Vegetable oil for deep frying		
Original Bisquick mix	2 cups	
Bisquick Gluten Free mix		2 cups
Unsweetened applesauce	⅓ cup	⅓ cup
Brown sugar, packed	2 tablespoons	2 tablespoons
Apple pie spice	1 teaspoon	1¾ teaspoons
Eggs		3
TOPPINGS		
Granulated sugar	½ cup	½ cup
Apple pie spice	1 teaspoon	1 teaspoon

Kitchen Secret: Store any remaining doughnuts in a covered container. Microwave 1 or 2 doughnuts on High for 10 seconds for a fresh-from-the-fryer taste.

Kitchen Secret: Be careful not to overcook these doughnuts as they become tough and dense. Fry just until golden brown.

1 In deep fryer or 3-quart saucepan, heat 2 to 3 inches of oil to 375°F.

2 Meanwhile, in medium bowl, stir Doughnut ingredients until well blended. Gather dough into a ball. Place dough on surface dusted with Bisquick mix; knead 10 to 12 times. Roll dough with rolling pin ½-inch thick. Cut with 3-inch doughnut cutter; reroll dough to make remaining doughnuts.

3 In gallon-size resealable food-storage plastic bag, combine Topping ingredients.

4 Carefully place 2 or 3 doughnuts at a time in hot oil. **Original:** Fry 1 to 1½ minutes, turning once, until golden brown. Using slotted spoon, remove doughnuts to paper towel–lined heatproof plate; cool 2 to 3 minutes. Place 3 to 4 doughnuts in bag; seal and shake to coat all sides. **Gluten Free:** Fry 30 to 60 seconds.

Original Applesauce Spice Doughnuts

CRAZY NIGHT SURVIVAL GUIDE

For those nights when you have no time, an empty pantry or you just don't feel like cooking—we have you covered.

- Sloppy joes or spaghetti? Create a list of your family's favorite, easy-to-prepare dinners and keep it inside your cupboard door or pantry to refer to when you're in a panic. Have the ingredients for those meals on hand so you can throw them together quickly.

- Scan your freezer, fridge and pantry for items that will fit one of these themes to create a meal:

  * **Bowls** Heat leftover rice or grains; pasta; any beans (legumes), such as black beans, kidney beans or navy beans; cut-up leftover cooked beef, pork, chicken or turkey; any cut-up cooked or fresh veggies; and any shredded or cubed cheese you have on hand. Spoon ingredients into premade waffle bowls (directions on page 101) or individual serving bowls.

  * **Breakfast** Serve your favorite breakfast foods, such as pancakes, waffles, eggs with bacon or sausage and toast, for dinner.

  * **Grilled Cheese** Use leftover pancakes, waffles or bread on hand. Layer other items such as cooked, chopped veggies, sliced pepperoni or sliced olives between thin slices of soft or medium-hard cheese, shredded cheese or cheese spread inside the pancakes, waffles or bread so that when the cheese melts, all the fillings stay in place.

  * **Pasta** Toss cooked pasta with butter and grated Parmesan, salad dressing, pasta sauce or barbecue sauce. Toss with leftover cut-up cooked beef, pork, chicken or turkey; cut-up salami or pepperoni slices; and any leftover, cut-up cooked veggies. You can reheat for a hot dish or serve cold as a salad.

  * **Sandwiches** Use leftover pancakes, waffles, bread, bagels or buns. Cold cuts, leftover meat or poultry can be sliced or shredded and layered with cheese slices, hummus or even peanut butter.

  * **Soup** Use leftover soup and add to it or make soup from leftover gravy (thin with water or milk), vegetable juice or broth. Add any leftover cooked pasta, grains or rice; leftover, cut-up cooked beef, pork, chicken or turkey; cut-up salami or pepperoni slices and any leftover cut-up cooked veggies. Simmer for a few minutes to blend flavors.

LOOK FOR THE RECIPES IN THIS BOOK THAT INDICATE:

- 15-minute prep
- 8 ingredients or less
- 30 minutes or less

Swim meet at 5:30 tonight!

DROP BISCUITS

| ORIGINAL: PREP TIME: 5 minutes | START TO FINISH: 15 minutes |
| GLUTEN FREE: PREP TIME: 10 minutes | START TO FINISH: 30 minutes |

	ORIGINAL	GLUTEN FREE
INGREDIENTS	Makes 9 biscuits	Makes 10 biscuits
Original Bisquick mix	2¼ cups	
Bisquick Gluten Free mix		2 cups
Shortening		⅓ cup
Eggs		3
Milk	⅔ cup	⅔ cup
TOPPINGS		
Butter		
Preserves/Gluten-free preserves		

1 Heat oven to 450°F. **Original:** Stir all ingredients until soft dough forms. **Gluten Free:** Place Bisquick Gluten Free mix in large bowl. Cut in shortening, using pastry blender or fork, until mixture is consistency of coarse crumbs. Stir in eggs with milk.

2 **Original:** Drop dough by 9 spoonfuls onto ungreased cookie sheet. **Gluten Free:** Drop dough by 10 spoonfuls onto ungreased cookie sheet.

3 **Original:** Bake 8 to 10 minutes or until golden brown. **Gluten Free:** Bake 13 to 16 minutes or until golden brown. Serve with Toppings.

Rolled Biscuits

After step 1, place dough on surface sprinkled with Bisquick mix; roll to coat. Shape into a ball; knead 10 times. Roll dough ½ inch thick. Cut with 2½-inch round cutter dipped in Bisquick mix. Place on ungreased cookie sheet. Continue as directed in step 3.

Gluten Free Drop Biscuits

15-minute prep
8 ingredients or less
30 minutes or less

CHEESE-GARLIC BISCUITS

ORIGINAL: PREP TIME: 5 minutes | START TO FINISH: 15 minutes

GLUTEN FREE: PREP TIME: 5 minutes | START TO FINISH: 15 minutes

INGREDIENTS	ORIGINAL Makes 9 biscuits	GLUTEN FREE Makes 10 biscuits
BISCUITS		
Original Bisquick mix	2 cups	
Bisquick Gluten Free mix		2 cups
Garlic powder		¼ teaspoon
Butter, cold		¼ cup
Milk	⅔ cup	⅔ cup
Shredded cheddar cheese	½ cup (2 oz)	½ cup gluten-free (2 oz)
Eggs		3
GARLIC-BUTTER TOPPING		
Butter, melted	2 tablespoons	¼ cup
Garlic powder	⅛ teaspoon	¼ teaspoon

Garlic-Cheese Breakfast Sandwiches

Cut warm biscuits horizontally in half, and fill with scrambled eggs and a slice of cheese.

1 **Original:** Heat oven to 450°F. **Gluten Free:** Heat oven to 425°F.

2 **Original:** In medium bowl, stir Bisquick mix, milk and cheese until soft dough forms. Drop dough by 9 spoonfuls onto ungreased cookie sheet. **Gluten Free:** In medium bowl, stir Gluten Free Bisquick mix and ¼ teaspoon garlic powder. Cut in ¼ cup butter, using pastry blender or fork, until mixture looks like coarse crumbs. Stir in milk, cheese and eggs until soft dough forms. Drop dough by 10 spoonfuls onto ungreased cookie sheet.

3 Bake 8 to 10 minutes or until golden brown.

4 Meanwhile, in small bowl, stir together Topping ingredients; brush over warm biscuits.

Original Cheese-Garlic
Biscuits

Original Italian Flatbread

ITALIAN FLATBREAD

ORIGINAL: PREP TIME: 15 minutes | START TO FINISH: 40 minutes

GLUTEN FREE: PREP TIME: 15 minutes | START TO FINISH: 40 minutes

INGREDIENTS	ORIGINAL	GLUTEN FREE
	Makes 1 flatbread (12 slices)	Makes 1 flatbread (12 slices)
Original Bisquick mix	2 cups	
Bisquick Gluten Free mix		1¾ cups
Very warm water (120°F to 130°F)	½ cup	⅔ cup
Vegetable oil		⅓ cup
Eggs, beaten		2
Butter, melted	2 tablespoons	2 tablespoons
Shredded cheddar cheese	¼ cup (1 oz)	¼ cup (1 oz)
Shredded Monterey Jack cheese	¼ cup (1 oz)	¼ cup (1 oz)
Grated Parmesan cheese	¼ cup	¼ cup
Parsley flakes	2 teaspoons	2 teaspoons
Italian seasoning	½ teaspoon	½ teaspoon

1 **Original:** Heat oven to 450°F. **Gluten Free:** Heat oven to 400°F.

2 **Original:** In medium bowl, stir Bisquick mix and water until stiff dough forms. Let stand 10 minutes. Place dough on surface generously sprinkled with Bisquick mix; gently roll in Bisquick mix to coat. Shape into ball; knead 60 times. **Gluten Free:** In medium bowl, stir Bisquick mix, water, oil and eggs until well blended. Do not knead.

3 Pat dough into 11-inch square on large ungreased cookie sheet, dusting fingers with Bisquick mix if necessary. Brush butter over dough. In small bowl, mix the cheeses, parsley flakes and seasoning; sprinkle over dough.

4 **Original:** Bake 10 to 12 minutes or until edges are light golden brown. **Gluten Free:** Bake 10 to 12 minutes or until cheese begins to brown and toothpick inserted in center comes out clean. Serve warm.

Kitchen Secret: You can use ½ cup pizza cheese blend instead of the cheddar and Monterey Jack cheeses.

Original Ultimate
Chicken Fingers

ULTIMATE CHICKEN FINGERS

	ORIGINAL: PREP TIME: 20 minutes	START TO FINISH: 35 minutes
	GLUTEN FREE: PREP TIME: 20 minutes	START TO FINISH: 35 minutes

INGREDIENTS	ORIGINAL	GLUTEN FREE
	Makes 4 servings	Makes 4 servings
Original Bisquick mix	⅔ cup	
Bisquick Gluten Free mix		¾ cup
Grated Parmesan cheese	½ cup	½ cup
Salt or garlic salt	½ teaspoon	½ teaspoon
Paprika	½ teaspoon	1 teaspoon
Eggs	1	2
Boneless, skinless chicken breast halves, cut crosswise into ½-inch strips	1 pound	1 pound
Butter, melted	3 tablespoons	3 tablespoons

1 Heat oven to 450°F. Line cookie sheet with foil; spray with cooking spray. **Gluten Free:** Use cooking spray without flour.

2 In shallow dish, mix Bisquick mix, cheese, salt and paprika. In another shallow dish, beat egg(s) slightly. Dip 1 or 2 chicken strips into egg(s), then coat with Bisquick mixture. Repeat dipping coated chicken in egg(s) and Bisquick mixture. Place chicken strips on cookie sheet. Drizzle butter over chicken.

3 Bake 12 to 14 minutes, turning after 6 minutes, until chicken is no longer pink in center.

EASY PIZZA

ORIGINAL: PREP TIME: 15 minutes | START TO FINISH: 30 minutes

GLUTEN FREE: PREP TIME: 10 minutes | START TO FINISH: 40 minutes

	ORIGINAL	GLUTEN FREE
INGREDIENTS	Makes 6 servings	Makes 6 servings
PIZZA CRUST		
Original Bisquick mix	1½ cups	
Bisquick Gluten Free mix		1⅓ cups
Very warm water (120°F to 130°F)	⅓ cup	½ cup
Italian seasoning, if desired	½ teaspoon	½ teaspoon
Vegetable oil		⅓ cup
Eggs, beaten		2
SUGGESTED TOPPINGS		
Pizza sauce	1 (8-oz) can	1 (8-oz) can
Pepperoni, sliced	1 (6-oz) package	1 (6-oz) package gluten-free
Bite-size vegetable pieces	1 cup	1 cup
Shredded mozzarella cheese	1½ cups (6 oz)	1½ cups gluten-free (6 oz)

1 Move oven rack to lowest position. Heat oven to 450°F. Grease or spray cookie sheet or 12-inch pizza pan with cooking spray. **Gluten Free:** Use cooking spray without flour.

2 **Original:** In medium bowl, mix all Pizza Crust ingredients; beat vigorously 20 strokes. Turn dough onto surface generously sprinkled with Bisquick mix; gently roll in baking mix to coat. Knead about 60 times or until smooth and no longer sticky. **Gluten Free:** Stir all Pizza Crust ingredients until well combined. Do not knead.

3 **Original:** Press dough into 12-inch round on cookie sheet with hands dusted with Bisquick mix; pinch edge, forming ½-inch rim. Or, press dough in pizza pan. **Gluten Free:** Spread in pan. Bake 15 minutes (crust will appear cracked).

4 Top with sauce, pepperoni and vegetables; sprinkle with cheese.

5 Bake 10 to 15 minutes or until cheese is melted.

Gluten Free Easy Pizza

IMPOSSIBLY EASY CHEESEBURGER PIE

ORIGINAL: PREP TIME: 15 minutes | START TO FINISH: 40 minutes

GLUTEN FREE: PREP TIME: 15 minutes | START TO FINISH: 45 minutes

	ORIGINAL	GLUTEN FREE
INGREDIENTS	Makes 6 servings	Makes 6 servings
Ground beef (at least 80% lean)	1 pound	1 pound
Onion, chopped	1 large (1 cup)	1 medium (½ cup)
Salt	½ teaspoon	½ teaspoon
Pepper		⅛ teaspoon
Shredded cheddar cheese	1 cup (4 oz)	1 cup gluten-free (4 oz)
Original Bisquick mix	½ cup	
Bisquick Gluten Free mix		½ cup
Milk	1 cup	1 cup
Eggs	2	3

1 Heat oven to 400°F. Spray 9-inch glass pie plate with cooking spray. **Gluten Free:** Use cooking spray without flour.

2 In 10-inch skillet, cook beef and onion over medium heat 8 to 10 minutes, stirring occasionally, until beef is browned; drain. Stir in salt. Spread in pie plate. Sprinkle with cheese. **Gluten Free:** Add pepper with salt.

3 In small bowl, stir remaining ingredients with fork or wire whisk until blended. Pour batter over ingredients in pie plate.

4 **Original:** Bake 23 to 25 minutes or until knife inserted in center comes out clean. Cut into wedges. **Gluten Free:** Bake 25 to 30 minutes. Let stand 5 minutes before serving.

Save Time: This can be prepared ahead; just cover and refrigerate up to 24 hours before baking. You may need to increase the bake time a few minutes.

Gluten Free Impossibly Easy Cheeseburger Pie

DUMPLINGS

ORIGINAL: PREP TIME: 5 minutes	START TO FINISH: 25 minutes	
GLUTEN FREE: PREP TIME: 5 minutes	START TO FINISH: 25 minutes	

INGREDIENTS	ORIGINAL Makes 10 dumplings	GLUTEN FREE Makes 8 dumplings
Original Bisquick mix	2 cups	
Bisquick Gluten Free mix		¾ cup
Milk	⅔ cup	⅓ cup
Butter, melted		2 tablespoons
Egg		1
Chopped fresh parsley	1 tablespoon (if desired)	1 tablespoon

1 In medium bowl, stir all ingredients until soft dough forms.

2 **Original:** Drop by 10 spoonfuls onto boiling stew; reduce heat. **Gluten Free:** Drop by 8 spoonfuls.

3 **Original:** Cook uncovered 10 minutes. Cover and cook 10 minutes. **Gluten Free:** Cook uncovered 10 minutes. Cover and cook 15 minutes.

Kitchen Secret: These dumplings can be used in any simmering stew. We've used them in Slow-Cooker Creamy Chicken and Herbed Dumplings (page 230).

Gluten Free Dumplings

Gluten Free Impossibly Easy French Apple Pie

IMPOSSIBLY EASY FRENCH APPLE PIE

ORIGINAL: PREP TIME: 25 minutes | START TO FINISH: 1 hour 15 minutes

GLUTEN FREE: PREP TIME: 25 minutes | START TO FINISH: 1 hour 25 minutes

INGREDIENTS	ORIGINAL	GLUTEN FREE
	Makes 6 servings	Makes 6 servings
FILLING		
Apples, peeled and sliced	3 cups (3 medium)	3 cups (3 medium)
Ground cinnamon	1 teaspoon	1 teaspoon
Ground nutmeg	¼ teaspoon	¼ teaspoon
Original Bisquick mix	½ cup	
Bisquick Gluten Free mix		½ cup
Granulated sugar	½ cup	½ cup
Milk	½ cup	½ cup
Butter, softened	1 tablespoon	1 tablespoon
Eggs	2	3
STREUSEL		
Original Bisquick mix	½ cup	
Bisquick Gluten Free mix		⅓ cup
Chopped nuts	¼ cup	⅓ cup
Brown sugar, packed	¼ cup	¼ cup
Butter, cold	2 tablespoons	3 tablespoons

1 Heat oven to 325°F. Spray 9-inch glass pie plate with cooking spray. **Gluten Free:** Use cooking spray without flour.

2 In medium bowl, mix apples, cinnamon and nutmeg; place in pie plate. In medium bowl, stir remaining Filling ingredients until well blended. Pour over apple mixture in pie plate. In small bowl, mix all Streusel ingredients until crumbly; sprinkle over filling.

3 **Original:** Bake 40 to 45 minutes or until knife inserted in center comes out clean. Let stand 5 minutes before serving. Cut into wedges. **Gluten Free:** Bake 45 to 50 minutes or until knife inserted in center comes out clean.

Save Time: Prepare as directed. Cover and refrigerate up to 24 hours before baking. You may need to increase the bake time a few minutes.

Kitchen Secret: If you have leftover pie, cover and store it in the refrigerator.

Gluten Free Velvet Crumb Cake

VELVET CRUMB CAKE

ORIGINAL: PREP TIME: 20 minutes | START TO FINISH: 1 hour

GLUTEN FREE: PREP TIME: 20 minutes | START TO FINISH: 1 hour

INGREDIENTS	ORIGINAL	GLUTEN FREE
	Makes 9 servings	Makes 9 servings
CAKE		
Original Bisquick mix	1½ cups	
Bisquick Gluten Free mix		1½ cups
Granulated sugar	½ cup	½ cup
Milk or water	½ cup	½ cup
Butter, softened	2 tablespoons	
Shortening		3 tablespoons
Vanilla	1 teaspoon	1 teaspoon gluten-free
Eggs	1	2
TOPPING		
Shredded coconut	½ cup	½ cup
Brown sugar, packed	⅓ cup	⅓ cup
Chopped nuts	¼ cup	¼ cup
Butter, softened	3 tablespoons	3 tablespoons
Milk	2 tablespoons	2 tablespoons

1 Heat oven to 350°F. Grease 8- or 9-inch square pan with shortening; lightly dust with Bisquick mix.

2 In large bowl, beat all Cake ingredients with electric mixer on low speed 30 seconds, scraping bowl constantly. Beat on medium speed 2 minutes, scraping bowl occasionally. Pour into pan.

3 **Original:** Bake 25 to 30 minutes or until toothpick inserted in center comes out clean. Cool 5 minutes. **Gluten Free:** Bake 22 to 27 minutes. Cool 5 minutes.

Continued on the next page

Continued from previous page

4 Set oven to broil. In small bowl, mix Topping ingredients. Spread topping evenly over cake to edge.

5 Broil cake with top about 3 inches from heat 1 to 2 minutes or until golden brown. Serve warm or cool completely.

Kitchen Secret: Perfectly bake this delightful cake by checking for doneness at the minimum time for the pan you've used, and add a minute or two if it isn't done yet. A broiled frosting is yummy and super quick; just watch it carefully under the broiler, as it can burn quickly.

Kitchen Secret: Mix in a handful of chocolate chips or butterscotch chips with the Topping ingredients for a decadent variation.

CLASSIC STRAWBERRY SHORTCAKES

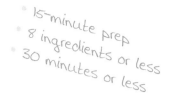

ORIGINAL: PREP TIME: 10 minutes | START TO FINISH: 30 minutes

GLUTEN FREE: PREP TIME: 10 minutes | START TO FINISH: 30 minutes

INGREDIENTS	ORIGINAL Makes 6 servings	GLUTEN FREE Makes 6 servings
Fresh strawberries, sliced	1 quart (4 cups)	1 quart (4 cups)
Sugar	¼ cup + 3 tablespoons	½ cup
Original Bisquick mix	2⅓ cups	
Bisquick Gluten Free mix		2⅓ cups
Milk	½ cup	¾ cup
Butter	3 tablespoons, melted	⅓ cup cold
Vanilla		½ teaspoon
Eggs		3
Sweetened Whipped Cream (page 276)	¾ cup	1½ cups

1 Heat oven to 425°F. **Gluten Free:** Grease or spray cookie sheet with cooking spray without flour.

2 In medium bowl, toss strawberries and ¼ cup of the sugar until coated; set aside.

3 **Original:** In medium bowl, stir Bisquick mix, remaining 3 tablespoons sugar, the milk and butter until soft dough forms. On ungreased cookie sheet, drop dough by 6 spoonfuls. **Gluten Free:** In medium bowl, stir Bisquick mix and remaining ¼ cup sugar. Cut in butter, using pastry blender or fork, until mixture looks like coarse crumbs. Stir in milk, vanilla and eggs. Drop dough by 6 spoonfuls onto cookie sheet.

4 **Original:** Bake 10 to 12 minutes or until golden brown. Cool 10 minutes. Using knife, split warm shortcakes. Fill and top with strawberries and whipped cream. **Gluten Free:** Bake 10 to 12 minutes or until light golden brown.

Kitchen Secret: For juicier berries, let the berry-sugar mixture stand an hour before assembling the shortcakes.

PANCAKE AND WAFFLE TIME

*15-minute prep
*8 ingredients or less

CHURRO PANCAKES

PREP TIME: 10 minutes | **START TO FINISH:** 40 minutes | Makes 6 servings (2 pancakes each)

2 tablespoons
vegetable oil

TOPPING
¼ cup sugar
1½ teaspoons
ground cinnamon

PANCAKES
2 cups Original
Bisquick mix
1 cup milk
1 teaspoon vanilla

1 Heat nonstick griddle to 300°F; brush with 1 tablespoon of the oil.

2 In small bowl, mix topping ingredients; reserve 2 tablespoons and set aside. In large bowl, mix remaining topping and the pancake ingredients until only a few lumps remain.

3 Spoon half the batter into quart-size resealable plastic bag; cut small tip from one end. Pipe batter onto hot griddle in 3- to 4-inch spirals starting at the center and working out, leaving about ¼ inch space between lines. Cook 30 to 60 seconds on each side or until lightly browned. Immediately sprinkle each pancake with 1 teaspoon of the reserved Topping.

4 Brush griddle with the remaining 1 tablespoon of the oil. Repeat with remaining batter and topping.

1 Serving Calories 250; Total Fat 8g (Saturated Fat 2g, Trans Fat 0g); Cholesterol 0mg; Sodium 400mg; Total Carbohydrate 39g (Dietary Fiber 1g); Protein 4g **Exchanges:** 1½ Starch, 1 Other Carbohydrate, 1½ Fat **Carbohydrate Choices:** 2½

Kitchen Secret: We suggest using a pastry brush for greasing the griddle. If you don't have a griddle, a 12-inch skillet will work, too, but it will take several batches to make all the pancakes. Cook over medium-low heat, and keep an eye on the heat to avoid overbrowning. Be sure to sprinkle the pancakes with the Topping while warm.

Kitchen Secret: The batter will thicken as it stands, so you may need to adjust the amount of space between the spirals as you pipe the batter.

Kitchen Secret: We loved these pancakes topped with the Cinnamon Smear (page 56). Spread pancakes with the butter mixture before sprinkling with Topping as directed. Another great way to serve them is to drizzle pancakes with chocolate or caramel ice-cream topping.

MINI GERMAN PANCAKE PUFFS WITH CINNAMON APPLES

PREP TIME: 20 minutes | START TO FINISH: 40 minutes | Makes 6 servings (2 pancake puffs each)

PANCAKE PUFFS

- 1 cup milk
- 2 tablespoons granulated sugar
- 1 teaspoon vanilla
- 3 eggs
- 1 cup Original Bisquick mix
- ¼ cup butter, melted

CINNAMON APPLES

- 3 medium Granny Smith apples, peeled, cut into ¼-inch pieces (3 cups)
- 6 tablespoons butter
- ½ cup packed light brown sugar
- 2 teaspoons ground cinnamon
- 1 cup apple cinnamon O-shaped whole-grain oat and corn cereal

1 Heat oven to 400°F. Spray 12 regular-size muffin cups with cooking spray.

2 In medium bowl, stir milk, granulated sugar, vanilla and eggs with whisk until smooth. Add Original Bisquick mix and ¼ cup butter; stir until smooth. Pour ¼ cup batter into each muffin cup.

3 Bake 15 to 17 minutes or until puffy and golden on top.

4 Meanwhile, in medium microwavable bowl, stir together apples, 6 tablespoons butter, the brown sugar and cinnamon. Microwave uncovered on High 3 to 5 minutes, stirring halfway through cooking time, until apples are soft. Cover to keep warm.

5 Cool pancake puffs 1 minute; remove from pan. To serve, place 2 puffs on each plate. Top with warm cinnamon apples and cereal.

1 Serving Calories 470; Total Fat 26g (Saturated Fat 14g, Trans Fat 1.5g); Cholesterol 145mg; Sodium 490mg; Total Carbohydrate 51g (Dietary Fiber 2g); Protein 7g **Exchanges:** 1 Starch, ½ Fruit, 2 Other Carbohydrate, ½ Medium-Fat Meat, 4½ Fat **Carbohydrate Choices:** 3½

Save Time: Be sure to cut the apples into ¼-inch pieces so that they will cook in the microwave in the time given. Bigger pieces will take longer.

Kitchen Secret: Serve the puffs with your favorite syrup, or make them extra special by adding a dollop of whipped cream sprinkled with cinnamon.

BLUEBERRY PANCAKE POPPERS

PREP TIME: 15 minutes | **START TO FINISH:** 30 minutes | Makes 24 poppers

PANCAKE POPPERS

- 1⅔ cups Original Bisquick mix
- ½ cup milk
- 2 tablespoons maple-flavored syrup
- 2 eggs
- 1 cup fresh or frozen (thawed) blueberries

CINNAMON SMEAR

- ¼ cup butter, softened
- 3 tablespoons maple-flavored syrup
- ¼ teaspoon ground cinnamon

1 Heat oven to 375°F. Spray 24 mini muffin cups with cooking spray.

2 In medium bowl, mix all Pancake Popper ingredients except the blueberries. Lightly fold half of the berries into the batter and divide evenly among muffin cups. Evenly divide remaining blueberries over batter.

3 Bake 10 to 12 minutes or until toothpick inserted in center comes out clean. Remove from muffin cups to cooling rack. Cool 5 minutes.

4 Meanwhile, in small bowl, stir together Cinnamon Smear ingredients. Spread butter mixture over tops of Pancake Poppers. Serve immediately.

1 Popper Calories 70; Total Fat 3g (Saturated Fat 1.5g, Trans Fat 0g); Cholesterol 20mg; Sodium 105mg; Total Carbohydrate 10g (Dietary Fiber 0g); Protein 1g **Exchanges:** ½ Starch, ½ Fat **Carbohydrate Choices:** ½

Kitchen Secret: Select smaller blueberries so more blueberries can be put in each mini muffin cup.

Kitchen Secret: Make these ahead for quick breakfasts on the go or a light snack. You can freeze the cooled Pancake Poppers in a resealable freezer storage bag. To reheat, place 4 poppers on microwavable plate. Cover with waxed paper. Heat on Medium (50%) power 1 minute 30 seconds to 2 minutes 30 seconds or until hot.

GLUTEN-FREE BUFFALO CHICKEN PANCAKE TACOS

PREP TIME: 30 minutes | **START TO FINISH:** 30 minutes | Makes 7 servings (2 tacos each)

1 Heat griddle or skillet over medium heat (350°F). Brush with vegetable oil, if necessary.

2 In large bowl, mix Pancake ingredients with whisk until blended.

3 For each pancake, pour about ¼ cup batter onto hot griddle. Cook 1 to 2 minutes or until edges are dry and bubbles begin to form on top. Turn; cook until golden brown. Place on heatproof plate and cover to keep warm until ready to serve.

4 In medium microwavable bowl, stir together shredded chicken and wing sauce. Cover; microwave on High 1 to 2 minutes or until hot, stirring once during cooking.

5 To assemble each taco, place ¼ cup buffalo chicken in center of warm pancake. Top with 1 tablespoon of the corn and about 2 tablespoons of the avocado. Drizzle with 1 tablespoon of the blue cheese dressing. Repeat with remaining pancakes and filling.

1 Serving Calories 540; Total Fat 34g (Saturated Fat 7g, Trans Fat 0g); Cholesterol 110mg; Sodium 980mg; Total Carbohydrate 35g (Dietary Fiber 2g); Protein 23g **Exchanges:** 1 Starch, 1½ Other Carbohydrate, 3 Lean Meat, 5 Fat **Carbohydrate Choices:** 2

Kitchen Secret: Use these ranch pancakes to make easy, flavorful sandwich roll-ups. Spread each pancake with a small amount of mayonnaise, top with sliced cheese and thinly sliced turkey or ham, and roll up.

Kitchen Secret: Love toppings? Top with chopped fresh cilantro leaves, chopped celery, shredded lettuce, more buffalo sauce or fresh pico de gallo.

PANCAKES
- 1½ cups Bisquick Gluten Free mix
- 1½ cups milk
- 3 tablespoons vegetable oil
- 2 tablespoons gluten-free ranch dressing mix (dry)
- 2 eggs

FILLING
- 3 cups shredded gluten-free rotisserie chicken
- ⅔ cup gluten-free buffalo wing sauce
- ¾ cup frozen roasted corn, cooked and drained
- 1 ripe avocado, peeled and chopped
- ¾ cup gluten-free blue cheese or ranch dressing

MINI FRENCH TOAST PANCAKES

PREP TIME: 25 minutes | **START TO FINISH:** 25 minutes | Makes 10 servings (5 pancakes each)

1 Heat griddle or 10-inch skillet over medium heat (350°F).

2 In medium bowl, stir ingredients with fork until blended.

3 For each pancake, pour 1 measuring tablespoon batter onto hot griddle. Cook about 1 minute or until bubbles break on surface and edges just begin to dry. Turn; cook until golden.

2 cups Original Bisquick mix

1½ cups French toast–flavored cereal, finely crushed to ¾ cup

1⅓ cups milk

½ teaspoon ground cinnamon

2 eggs

1 Serving Calories 160; Total Fat 6g (Saturated Fat 1.5g, Trans Fat 0.5g); Cholesterol 40mg; Sodium 350mg; Total Carbohydrate 22g (Dietary Fiber 0g); Protein 4g **Exchanges:** 1 Starch, ½ Other Carbohydrate, 1 Fat **Carbohydrate Choices:** 1½

Kitchen Secret: Try these mini pancakes topped with syrup, additional cereal and fresh fruit, or with yogurt, honey, sliced strawberries and bananas.

Kitchen Secret: These little pancakes are perfect for tiny hands! They are easy to pick up and nibble on or to dip before devouring.

LEMON SOUFFLÉ PANCAKE

PREP TIME: 15 minutes | **START TO FINISH:** 40 minutes | Makes 6 servings

PANCAKE

- 1 teaspoon butter
- 2 eggs, separated
- 1½ cups Original Bisquick mix
- 2 tablespoons sugar
- ½ cup milk
- 1 tablespoon grated lemon zest
- 2 tablespoons lemon juice

TOPPINGS

- 2 tablespoons lemon curd (from 10-oz jar)
- ¼ cup fresh raspberries or blueberries

1. Heat oven to 350°F. Heat ovenproof 8-inch nonstick skillet over medium heat; melt butter in skillet. Swirl to coat bottom and side of pan; remove from heat.

2. In medium bowl, beat egg whites with electric mixer on high speed until foamy. Continue beating until stiff peaks form and mixture is glossy, about 1 minute; set aside.

3. In medium bowl, stir together Original Bisquick mix and sugar. In small bowl, mix milk, lemon zest, lemon juice and egg yolks until blended; add to Bisquick mix and stir until blended. Gently fold egg whites into batter; pour batter into skillet.

4. Bake 17 to 20 minutes or until center springs back when touched in center and pancake pulls away from sides. Let stand 5 minutes. Carefully run spatula around sides of pan.

5. Turn skillet over onto heatproof serving plate. Top pancake with lemon curd and berries. Cut into 6 wedges.

1 Serving Calories 200; Total Fat 5g (Saturated Fat 2g, Trans Fat 0g); Cholesterol 70mg; Sodium 330mg; Total Carbohydrate 31g (Dietary Fiber 1g); Protein 5g **Exchanges:** 1 Starch, 1 Other Carbohydrate, 1 Fat **Carbohydrate Choices:** 2

Kitchen Secret: Using a nonstick pan produces a pancake with a lovely golden-brown color. Using a regular pan also works but gives the pancake a pale yellow color.

Kitchen Secret: This unique pancake incorporates whipped egg whites to give it a lighter texture, more like that of a soufflé, but with the delicious taste of a pancake. If you like, top it with lemon wedges in addition to the berries or serve with Sweetened Whipped Cream (page 276) for a lovely complement to the lemon flavor.

15-minute prep
30 minutes or less

GLUTEN-FREE OATMEAL PANCAKES

PREP TIME: 10 minutes | **START TO FINISH:** 20 minutes | Makes 7 servings (3 pancakes each)

OATMEAL PANCAKES

2	cups Bisquick Gluten Free mix
2	cups milk
¼	cup vegetable oil
2	teaspoons vanilla
2	eggs
⅓	cup gluten-free quick-cooking oats

TOPPINGS

2	cups fresh blueberries
½	cup unsweetened large coconut flakes, toasted
1¼	cups real maple syrup

1 Heat griddle or 10-inch skillet over medium-high heat (375°F).

2 In medium bowl, stir Bisquick Gluten Free mix, milk, oil, vanilla and eggs until blended. Stir in oats. Pour slightly less than ¼ cup batter onto hot griddle.

3 Cook about 2 minutes or until bubbles break on surface and edges just begin to dry. Turn; cook until golden. Serve with blueberries, coconut and maple syrup.

1 Serving Calories 340; Total Fat 9g (Saturated Fat 3g, Trans Fat 0g); Cholesterol 40mg; Sodium 310mg; Total Carbohydrate 59g (Dietary Fiber 1g); Protein 5g **Exchanges:** 1½ Starch, 2½ Other Carbohydrate, 1½ Fat **Carbohydrate Choices:** 4

Kitchen Secret: Turn pancakes only once as repeated cooking on both sides toughens rather than browns the pancakes.

Kitchen Secret: To toast coconut, heat in ungreased heavy skillet over medium-low heat 6 to 14 minutes, stirring frequently until browning begins, then stirring constantly until golden brown.

LUSCIOUS BROWNIE PANCAKE STACKS

PREP TIME: 30 minutes | **START TO FINISH:** 30 minutes | Makes 6 servings (3 pancakes each)

2	cups Original Bisquick mix
1¼	cups milk
½	cup unsweetened baking cocoa
¼	cup sugar
¼	cup butter, melted
1	teaspoon vanilla
¼	teaspoon salt
2	eggs
½	cup hazelnut spread with cocoa
2	cups fresh raspberries

1 Heat nonstick griddle or skillet over medium-low heat (300°F). Brush with vegetable oil, if necessary.

2 In medium bowl, stir Original Bisquick mix, milk, cocoa, sugar, butter, vanilla, salt and eggs with whisk until well blended.

3 For each pancake, scoop generous ¼ cup batter onto hot griddle. Cook about 1 minute or until bubbly on top and dry around edges. Turn; cook until light golden brown.

4 To assemble each pancake stack, place one pancake on serving plate. Spread with generous 1 teaspoon hazelnut spread. Top with another pancake. Top with generous 1 teaspoon hazelnut spread and another pancake. Spread or drizzle generous 1 teaspoon hazelnut spread over top of stack. Top each pancake stack with about ⅓ cup raspberries.

1 Serving Calories 490; Total Fat 22g (Saturated Fat 8g, Trans Fat 0g); Cholesterol 85mg; Sodium 600mg; Total Carbohydrate 63g (Dietary Fiber 7g); Protein 10g **Exchanges:** 1 Starch, ½ Fruit, 2½ Other Carbohydrate, 1 High-Fat Meat, 2½ Fat **Carbohydrate Choices:** 4

Save Time: If you don't want to make all pancake stacks at once, pancakes can be frozen and reheated in the microwave. To freeze, cool pancakes completely on cooling rack. Transfer cooled pancakes to freezer food storage bag and store in freezer. To reheat, place 3 pancakes on microwavable plate. Cover loosely with a paper towel. Microwave on High 30 seconds to 45 seconds or until heated through.

Kitchen Secret: For a different look, the hazelnut spread can be drizzled over the top of the pancake stack. Warm the hazelnut spread slightly in the microwave until drizzling consistency. You can also sprinkle raspberries with powdered sugar.

*8 ingredients or less
*30 minutes or less

GLAZED DOUGHNUT PANCAKES

PREP TIME: 20 minutes | **START TO FINISH:** 20 minutes | Makes 14 pancakes

1 Heat griddle or skillet over medium-high heat (375°F). Brush griddle with vegetable oil if necessary.

2 In medium bowl, stir Pancake ingredients until blended. Place batter in resealable plastic bag; cut ½ inch from bottom corner of bag.

3 For each doughnut pancake, squeeze batter from bag onto hot griddle into 4-inch circle, leaving hole in center. Cook 30 to 60 seconds or until bubbly on top and dry around the edges. Turn pancakes; cook until golden brown.

4 Meanwhile, in small bowl, stir Pancake Glaze ingredients, except sprinkles, until smooth; set aside.

5 Spread tops of warm pancakes with Pancake Glaze. Sprinkle with sprinkles. Serve immediately.

PANCAKES

2	cups Original Bisquick mix
¾	cup milk
1	tablespoon granulated sugar
2	eggs

PANCAKE GLAZE

1½	cups powdered sugar
3	tablespoons butter, melted
2	tablespoons milk
1	teaspoon vanilla
1	tablespoon candy sprinkles

1 Pancake Calories 170; Total Fat 5g (Saturated Fat 2.5g, Trans Fat 0g); Cholesterol 35mg; Sodium 200mg; Total Carbohydrate 27g (Dietary Fiber 0g); Protein 2g **Exchanges:** 1 Starch, 1 Other Carbohydrate, 1 Fat **Carbohydrate Choices:** 2

Kitchen Secret: If the pancake batter spreads too much, it may be helpful to first pipe a thin 4-inch circle of batter onto hot griddle. Then pipe another thicker layer of batter over the first.

Kitchen Secret: Got just a little batter left? Make adorable doughnut minis! Drizzle with caramel topping.

QUINOA-SEED PANCAKES
<u>WITH</u> MIXED BERRY SYRUP

PREP TIME: 20 minutes | START TO FINISH: 20 minutes | Makes 5 servings (3 pancakes each + ¼ cup syrup)

1 In 2-quart saucepan, cook Mixed Berry Syrup ingredients over medium heat (350°F), stirring occasionally and breaking up large berries with spoon, until berries are thawed and syrup is hot. Remove from heat; set aside.

2 Heat griddle or skillet to medium-high heat (375°F). Brush griddle with vegetable oil if necessary.

3 Meanwhile, in medium bowl, stir Original Bisquick mix, milk, oats, quinoa, chia seeds, flaxseed and eggs until well blended.

4 For each pancake, pour slightly less than ¼ cup batter onto hot griddle. Cook pancakes 1 to 2 minutes or until bubbly on top and dry around edges. Turn; cook until golden brown.

5 Serve pancakes with Mixed Berry Syrup.

1 Serving Calories 360; Total Fat 9g (Saturated Fat 2.5g, Trans Fat 0g); Cholesterol 80mg; Sodium 330mg; Total Carbohydrate 60g (Dietary Fiber 6g); Protein 9g **Exchanges:** 1½ Starch, ½ Fruit, 2 Other Carbohydrate, 1 Medium-Fat Meat, ½ Fat **Carbohydrate Choices:** 4

Kitchen Secret: No bags of mixed berries in your freezer? Make your own berry combinations with frozen blueberries and raspberries or strawberries.

Kitchen Secret: Serve pancakes with a dollop of Sweetened Whipped Cream (page 276). Stir additional chia seeds into the whipped cream for an extra boost of fiber.

MIXED BERRY SYRUP
- 1¼ cups frozen mixed berries (from 12- to 15-oz bag)
- ½ cup maple-flavored syrup

PANCAKES
- 1 cup Original Bisquick mix
- 1 cup milk
- ½ cup old-fashioned or quick-cooking oats
- ½ cup cooked quinoa
- 2 tablespoons chia seeds
- 2 tablespoons whole flaxseed
- 2 eggs

SWEETHEART PANCAKES

PREP TIME: 20 minutes | START TO FINISH: 20 minutes | Makes 5 servings (2 pancakes each)

2 cups Original
  Bisquick mix
1 cup milk
1 tablespoon sugar
2 eggs
1 teaspoon red liquid
  food color

1 Heat griddle or 10-inch skillet over medium-high heat (375°F).

2 In large bowl, stir Original Bisquick mix, milk, sugar and eggs with whisk until well blended. Divide batter between 2 medium bowls; stir food color into 1 bowl.

3 For each pancake, starting with the white batter, pour ¼ cup batter onto hot griddle. Cook 2 to 3 minutes or until bubbles break on surface on top and edges just begin to dry. Turn; cook other side until golden brown. Repeat with red batter.

4 Using 3- to 3½-inch heart-shaped cookie cutter, cut one shape from each warm pancake. Place cutout shapes on opposite color pancakes.

1 Serving Calories 270; Total Fat 10g (Saturated Fat 3g, Trans Fat 1g); Cholesterol 80mg; Sodium 640mg; Total Carbohydrate 36g (Dietary Fiber 1g); Protein 7g **Exchanges:** 2½ Starch, 1½ Fat **Carbohydrate Choices:** 2½

Save Time: Rather than having you count out maybe a hundred drops of food color, we make it easier by calling for a teaspoon amount to cut your time in the kitchen.

Kitchen Secret: If you like, you can serve these up with just syrup, dust with powdered sugar and drizzle with syrup or sprinkle them with powdered sugar and candy sprinkles.

JALAPEÑO-CHEDDAR SHEET PAN PANCAKES

PREP TIME: 20 minutes | **START TO FINISH:** 50 minutes | Makes 8 servings (2 pancakes + 1 tablespoon topping each)

½ cup thinly sliced green onion

½ cup sour cream

1½ teaspoons taco seasoning mix (from 1-oz package)

1 cup sliced drained roasted red peppers (from 16-oz jar)

2 cups Original Bisquick mix

½ cup cornmeal

2 cups milk

1 cup shredded cheddar cheese (4 oz)

½ cup butter, melted

2 eggs, slightly beaten

2 small fresh jalapeño chiles, thinly sliced

1 Heat oven to 400°F. Spray 15 × 10 × 1-inch pan with cooking spray.

2 In small bowl, mix 2 tablespoons of the green onion, the sour cream and taco seasoning mix; cover and refrigerate until serving time. Chop ½ cup of the red peppers; set aside.

3 In large bowl, stir Original Bisquick mix and cornmeal until blended. In medium bowl, beat the chopped roasted red pepper, milk, cheddar cheese, butter, eggs and remaining green onion until blended. Stir egg mixture into Bisquick mixture until just blended (batter may be lumpy).

4 Pour into pan. Arrange reserved red pepper strips and jalapeño slices on top.

5 Bake 18 to 22 minutes or until golden brown and toothpick inserted in center comes out clean. Cool on cooling rack 10 minutes. Cut into 4 rows by 4 rows. Serve sour cream mixture with pancakes.

1 Serving Calories 400; Total Fat 24g (Saturated Fat 13g, Trans Fat 1g); Cholesterol 105mg; Sodium 720mg; Total Carbohydrate 37g (Dietary Fiber 1g); Protein 10g **Exchanges:** 1 Starch, 1½ Other Carbohydrate, ½ Medium-Fat Meat, ½ High-Fat Meat, 3½ Fat **Carbohydrate Choices:** 2½

Kitchen Secret: Jalapeño chiles come in a wide variety of sizes. If you have a large chile, use 1 and halve the larger slices. We suggest leaving the seeds in for pancakes with some heat. For a milder taste, carefully remove the seeds from the slices before adding to the top of the pancake.

Kitchen Secret: Savory pancakes? Why not! If you're not a fan of sweet pancakes, give this one a try. Sprinkle with sliced green onions or top with sliced jalapeños. Serve them with chorizo or breakfast sausage, refried or pinto beans or cooked bacon as a delicious accompaniment.

BERRIES AND CREAM DUTCH BABY

PREP TIME: 15 minutes | **START TO FINISH:** 40 minutes | Makes 6 servings

⅓ cup water

2 tablespoons butter

½ cup Original Bisquick mix

2 eggs

1 oz (from 8-oz package) cream cheese, softened

¼ cup heavy whipping cream

2 teaspoons powdered sugar

1 teaspoon grated lemon zest

2 cups assorted fresh berries (raspberries, blueberries, blackberries and strawberries)

2 tablespoons honey

1 Heat oven to 400°F. Generously spray 9-inch glass pie plate with cooking spray.

2 In 2-quart saucepan, heat water and butter to boiling. Add Original Bisquick mix; stir vigorously over low heat about 1 minute or until mixture forms a ball. Remove from heat.

3 With spoon, beat in eggs, one at a time, beating until smooth and glossy after each addition. Spread in bottom of pie plate (do not spread up sides).

4 Bake 20 to 25 minutes or until puffed, dry in center and deep golden brown.

5 Meanwhile, in small bowl, beat cream cheese, whipping cream, powdered sugar and lemon zest with electric mixer on medium speed 1 to 2 minutes or until soft peaks form.

6 Remove Dutch Baby from oven. Immediately top with berries and cream cheese topping. Drizzle with honey. Serve immediately.

1 Serving Calories 200; Total Fat 12g (Saturated Fat 6g, Trans Fat 0g); Cholesterol 85mg; Sodium 190mg; Total Carbohydrate 19g (Dietary Fiber 2g); Protein 3g **Exchanges:** ½ Starch, ½ Fruit, ½ Other Carbohydrate, 2½ Fat **Carbohydrate Choices:** 1

Kitchen Secret: Be sure to beat in the eggs one at a time, as directed in the recipe, to get the best-looking puffy Dutch Baby.

Save Time: We know you don't want to spend all day in the kitchen, so wherever it's easily feasible, we try to have you doing two things at one time so that you get to the eating part faster! Look for the word *meanwhile* to show you what you can do to save time on the recipe.

5 CREATIVE BREAKFASTS ON THE GO

Sometimes it's hard to get out the door in the morning . . . or every day, if you're a sleepyhead. Wake up and start a great day with one of these quick, satisfying breakfasts. See page 11 for how to store and reheat pancakes and waffles so these meals are superfast to put together.

CAKEADILLAS Make quesadillas with leftover pancakes, loading them with shredded cheese and scrambled eggs, leftover cooked veggies and cooked bacon. Or make with peanut butter and jelly—amazing!

PANCAKE TACOS Hold a pancake in your hand and fill it with cut-up fresh fruit, yogurt and granola on top for a little crunch.

WAFFLE TAQUITOS Flatten waffles with a rolling pin and top with a thin layer of guacamole or spreadable cream cheese, scrambled eggs and shredded cheese; roll up and wrap in waxed paper.

BENTO BREAKFASTS Fill food bento boxes with mini pancakes or waffle sticks and syrup, bite-size pieces of fruit and cheese cubes or nuts.

HAM AND CHEESE NAAN Use Quick Lemon-Rosemary Naan (page 179) cut in half as the bread (or pancakes); spread it with pimiento cheese, your favorite mustard or spreadable cream cheese. Top with deli ham and cheese slices and a fried egg before adding the top half of the naan.

TURKEY CLUB PANCAKE PANINI

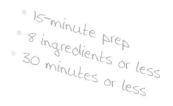

15-minute prep
8 ingredients or less
30 minutes or less

PREP TIME: 10 minutes | START TO FINISH: 15 minutes | Makes 4 sandwiches

1 Heat panini maker.

2 In small bowl, stir together butter and garlic powder. Spread on one side of each pancake.

3 Place 4 pancakes, butter side down, on work surface. Divide cheese, tomato, turkey and avocado among pancakes. Top with remaining pancakes, butter side up.

4 Place 2 sandwiches on panini maker. Close lid, pressing to flatten sandwiches; cook 2 to 3 minutes or until sandwiches are toasted and cheese is melted. Repeat with remaining sandwiches.

2	tablespoons butter, softened
¼	teaspoon garlic powder
8	Classic Pancakes (page 16)
4	slices (¾ oz each) cheddar cheese
4	slices tomato
8	oz thinly sliced, cooked deli turkey breast
1	avocado, peeled and sliced

1 Sandwich Calories 430; Total Fat 25g (Saturated Fat 11g, Trans Fat 0g); Cholesterol 120mg; Sodium 1,220mg; Total Carbohydrate 32g (Dietary Fiber 3g); Protein 21g **Exchanges:** 1½ Starch, ½ Other Carbohydrate, 2 Lean Meat, ½ High-Fat Meat, 3 Fat **Carbohydrate Choices:** 2

Kitchen Secret: Pancakes can be the start of other great paninis, too! Try roast beef, Swiss cheese and sliced onion or ham and Colby–Monterey Jack cheese.

Save Time: Freeze leftover pancakes to use in recipes like this one or to have on hand when you are out of fresh bread.

EGG AND SAUSAGE PANCAKE CUPS

PREP TIME: 25 minutes | START TO FINISH: 40 minutes | Makes 6 servings (2 cups each)

1 Heat oven to 375°F. Spray 12 regular-size muffin cups with cooking spray.

2 In large bowl, stir together Original Bisquick mix, spinach, milk, chives and 1 of the eggs. Spoon generous 1 tablespoon batter into bottom of each muffin cup.

3 In medium bowl, beat remaining eggs, water, salt and pepper until well blended. In 10-inch nonstick skillet, melt butter over medium heat. Add egg mixture; cook 2 to 3 minutes, stirring occasionally, until firm but still moist. Stir in hash browns, sausage and cheese; cook about 1 minute or until cheese is melted. Divide egg mixture among cups (slightly less than 2 tablespoons each).

4 Bake 9 to 11 minutes or until light brown and toothpick inserted in pancake cup comes out clean. Let stand 5 minutes.

1 Serving Calories 200; Total Fat 11g (Saturated Fat 4.5g, Trans Fat 0g); Cholesterol 140mg; Sodium 470mg; Total Carbohydrate 17g (Dietary Fiber 0g); Protein 8g **Exchanges:** ½ Starch, ½ Other Carbohydrate, ½ Medium-Fat Meat, ½ High-Fat Meat, 1 Fat **Carbohydrate Choices:** 1

Kitchen Secret: There are lots of options for these tasty breakfast cups! You can use an equal amount of cooked sausage, bacon or ground beef in place of the frozen sausage crumbles or omit the meat, if you like. You can also change up the cheese by substituting shredded pizza cheese or cheddar cheese or swap green onions or red onion for the chives.

Kitchen Secret: Sprinkle cups with additional chopped chives, if you like.

Save Time: These hearty pancake cups can be made ahead for a quick breakfast. Prepare as directed; cool. Freeze in resealable plastic freezer bag or a covered container. To heat, place 2 pancake cups on a microwavable plate. Microwave on Medium (50%) 2 to 3 minutes or until hot.

1 cup Original Bisquick mix

½ cup chopped fresh spinach leaves

⅓ cup milk

1 tablespoon chopped fresh chives

4 eggs

1 tablespoon water

¼ teaspoon salt

⅛ teaspoon pepper

1 tablespoon butter

⅓ cup refrigerated hash brown potatoes (from 20-oz bag)

⅓ cup frozen cooked sausage crumbles, thawed (from 9.6-oz package)

⅓ cup shredded Italian blend cheese

TURTLE SHEET PAN PANCAKES

PREP TIME: 20 minutes | START TO FINISH: 35 minutes | Makes 8 servings (3 pancakes each)

¾ cup chopped pecans

3 tablespoons butter, melted

⅛ teaspoon fine sea salt

2 cups Original Bisquick mix

1 cup milk

¼ cup sugar

2 eggs, slightly beaten

½ cup miniature semisweet chocolate chips

Sweetened Whipped Cream (1½ cups), page 276

8 teaspoons caramel sauce

8 teaspoons chocolate sauce

1 Heat oven to 400°F. Line cookie sheet with foil. Spray 15 × 10 × 1-inch pan with cooking spray.

2 In small bowl, mix pecans and 1 tablespoon of the melted butter. Spread on cookie sheet. Sprinkle with salt. Bake for 4 to 5 minutes or until golden brown. Cool 5 minutes.

3 In large bowl, mix Original Bisquick, 2 tablespoons of the remaining melted butter, the milk, sugar and eggs with whisk until blended. Spread into pan. Sprinkle with chocolate chips and ½ cup of the toasted pecans.

4 Bake 12 to 15 minutes or until golden brown and toothpick inserted in center comes out clean.

5 To serve, cut into 6 rows by 4 rows. For each serving, place 3 pancakes on individual serving plate. Top with a dollop of Sweetened Whipped Cream. Drizzle each with 1 teaspoon caramel and 1 teaspoon chocolate sauce. Sprinkle with remaining toasted pecans. Serve immediately.

1 Serving Calories 450; Total Fat 26g (Saturated Fat 11g, Trans Fat 0g); Cholesterol 85mg; Sodium 420mg; Total Carbohydrate 47g (Dietary Fiber 2g); Protein 7g **Exchanges:** ½ Starch, 2½ Other Carbohydrate, 1 High-Fat Meat, 3½ Fat **Carbohydrate Choices:** 3

Kitchen Secret: Turtle is a name that describes the flavor combination of chocolate, nuts and caramel. It started with a popular turtle-shaped candy developed in the early 1900s with this unbeatable flavor combination.

Kitchen Secret: This recipe calls for fine sea salt. Sea salt has a milder salty taste than table salt. Table salt can be used in place of the sea salt, but the saltiness will be a bit more intense.

Save Time: Short on time? Refrigerated whipped cream in a can or frozen whipped topping, thawed, can be used in place of the Sweetened Whipped Cream.

FRUIT-TOPPED CITRUS WAFFLES

PREP TIME: 45 minutes | START TO FINISH: 45 minutes | 8 servings (1 waffle + ¼ cup fruit compote)

FRUIT COMPOTE

- 2 tablespoons honey
- 1 tablespoon fresh orange juice
- 1 tablespoon fresh lime juice
- 1 medium mango, chopped
- 2 cups fresh berries, such as blueberries, raspberries and sliced strawberries

WAFFLES

- 2 cups Original Bisquick mix
- 1¼ cups milk
- 2 tablespoons sugar
- 2 tablespoons vegetable oil
- 2 tablespoons lemon juice
- 2 teaspoons baking powder
- 1 teaspoon grated lemon zest
- 1 teaspoon grated orange zest
- ½ teaspoon grated lime zest
- 1 egg

1 In medium bowl, stir honey, orange juice and lime juice until smooth. Stir in mango and berries until coated; set aside.

2 Brush waffle maker with vegetable oil or spray with cooking spray. Heat waffle maker.

3 In medium bowl, stir Waffle ingredients with whisk until blended. For each waffle, pour about ½ cup batter onto center of hot waffle maker. Close lid of waffle maker. Bake 3 to 4 minutes or until waffles are golden brown. Carefully remove waffle to cooling rack; repeat with remaining batter.

4 Top waffles with Fruit Compote.

1 Serving Calories 250; Total Fat 7g (Saturated Fat 2g, Trans Fat 0g); Cholesterol 25mg; Sodium 430mg; Total Carbohydrate 42g (Dietary Fiber 2g); Protein 5g **Exchanges:** 1 Starch, 1 Fruit, 1 Other Carbohydrate, 1½ Fat **Carbohydrate Choices:** 3

Kitchen Secret: Garnish waffles with a dollop of vanilla or plain yogurt and a citrus peel.

Kitchen Secret: Citrus trees are native to southeast Asia and include oranges, lemons, limes, grapefruit, tangerines and pummelos. The fruit is characterized by internal segments separated by edible skin. The exterior skin contains aromatic oils, so when the skin is zested, the oils from the zest add wonderful citrus flavor to foods. It works best to zest the fruit before squeezing the juice.

ORANGE-WALNUT WAFFLES

PREP TIME: 20 minutes | START TO FINISH: 20 minutes | Makes 6 waffles

WAFFLES

- 2 cups Original Bisquick mix
- 1⅓ cups milk
- ½ cup chopped walnuts
- ⅓ cup orange marmalade
- 1 egg

ORANGE-MAPLE SYRUP

- ⅓ cup maple-flavored syrup
- 3 tablespoons orange marmalade

1 Brush waffle maker with vegetable oil or spray with cooking spray. Heat waffle maker.

2 In medium bowl, stir together Waffle ingredients until blended. Pour ½ cup batter onto center of hot waffle maker. Close lid of waffle maker.

3 Bake 1½ to 2 minutes or until waffle is golden brown. Carefully remove waffle to cooling rack; repeat with remaining batter.

4 In small saucepan, heat Syrup ingredients until hot. Serve syrup over waffles.

1 **Waffle** Calories 390; Total Fat 11g (Saturated Fat 2.5g, Trans Fat 0g); Cholesterol 35mg; Sodium 440mg; Total Carbohydrate 63g (Dietary Fiber 2g); Protein 7g **Exchanges:** 1 Starch, 3 Other Carbohydrate, ½ High-Fat Meat, 1½ Fat **Carbohydrate Choices:** 4

Kitchen Secret: Waffle makers come in a variety of shapes and sizes, so you may need to adjust the amount of batter for your waffle maker. Depending on the size and shape of your waffle maker, you may yield more or fewer waffles.

Kitchen Secret: Spoon whipped cream, walnuts and orange zest on the waffles after drizzling with syrup. It's like eating an over-the-top creamsicle!

CARAMEL UPSIDE-DOWN FRENCH TOAST

PREP TIME: 15 minutes | **START TO FINISH:** 55 minutes | Makes 8 servings

1 Heat oven to 350°F.

2 In medium bowl, beat eggs. Add milk, Original Bisquick mix and cinnamon and whisk together until blended. Place slices of bread, cut side down, in single layer in 13 × 9-inch (3-quart) glass baking dish. Pour egg mixture over slices. Let stand 5 minutes.

3 Meanwhile, in 10-inch ovenproof skillet, melt butter over medium-low heat; remove from heat. Stir in brown sugar until well blended. Turn each slice over, and place cut side down in bottom of skillet, fitting slices tightly together and tearing to fit empty spots between slices. Discard remaining egg mixture.

4 Bake 25 to 30 minutes or until edges are bubbly and top of toast is golden brown. Cool skillet on cooling rack 5 minutes.

5 Run metal spatula around edges to loosen. Place heatproof serving plate upside down over skillet; turn plate and skillet over. Remove skillet, scraping any extra caramel from bottom of skillet onto French toast. Serve immediately.

3	eggs
¾	cup milk
¼	cup Original Bisquick mix
¾	teaspoon ground cinnamon
10	slices (1 inch thick) French bread
⅓	cup butter
⅓	cup packed brown sugar

1 Serving Calories 380; Total Fat 12g (Saturated Fat 6g, Trans Fat 0g); Cholesterol 90mg; Sodium 610mg; Total Carbohydrate 55g (Dietary Fiber 2g); Protein 12g **Exchanges:** 3 Starch, ½ Other Carbohydrate, ½ Medium-Fat Meat, 1½ Fat **Carbohydrate Choices:** 3½

Kitchen Secret: Use a serrated bread knife to easily cut bread slices. Save the loaf ends for another use so each slice will readily soak up egg mixture.

Kitchen Secret: For a bit of decadence, serve with caramel ice-cream topping and fresh berries.

RASPBERRY AND HONEY RICOTTA WAFFLES

PREP TIME: 30 minutes | **START TO FINISH:** 30 minutes | Makes 6 waffles

1. Brush waffle maker with vegetable oil or spray with cooking spray. Heat waffle maker.

2. In medium bowl, combine all Waffle ingredients except raspberries until blended. Fold in raspberries.

3. Pour ½ cup waffle batter onto center of hot waffle maker. Spread slightly; close lid of waffle maker.

4. Bake for 2 to 3 minutes or until waffle is golden brown. Carefully remove waffle to cooling rack; repeat with remaining batter.

5. To serve, cut each waffle into quarters. Arrange quarters on serving plate. Top with 1 tablespoon of the ricotta cheese and fresh raspberries; drizzle with honey. Serve immediately.

1 Waffle Calories 350; Total Fat 12g (Saturated Fat 5g, Trans Fat 0g); Cholesterol 80mg; Sodium 440mg; Total Carbohydrate 49g (Dietary Fiber 3g); Protein 10g **Exchanges:** 1 Starch, ½ Fruit, 2 Other Carbohydrate, 1 High-Fat Meat, ½ Fat **Carbohydrate Choices:** 3

Kitchen Secret: Ricotta cheese is a fresh cheese, not an aged cheese, which gives it its light, moist, creamy texture. It is often used as a substitute for cream cheese in recipes. We like whole milk ricotta in this recipe for its richer flavor and texture compared to lower-fat varieties.

Kitchen Secret: Love blueberries? Use them in place of the raspberries. You can also sprinkle the waffles with powdered sugar, if you like. Spoon into a fine-mesh strainer and tap the edge of the strainer lightly over the waffles.

WAFFLES
- 2 cups Original Bisquick mix
- ½ cup whole milk ricotta cheese (from 15-oz container)
- ½ cup milk
- 2 tablespoons honey
- 1 tablespoon vegetable oil
- 2 eggs
- 1 cup fresh raspberries, slightly broken apart

TOPPINGS
- 6 tablespoons whole milk ricotta cheese
- ¾ cup fresh raspberries
- 3 tablespoons honey

SUNNY BREAKFAST WAFFLE-WICHES

PREP TIME: 25 minutes | START TO FINISH: 25 minutes | Makes 6 sandwiches

½ medium orange or yellow bell pepper, cut into 12 strips

6 slices prosciutto

1 medium ripe avocado

¼ cup mayonnaise or salad dressing

1 tablespoon lemon or lime juice

½ teaspoon salt

¼ teaspoon pepper

2 tablespoons vegetable oil

6 eggs

6 Classic Waffles (page 18), halved and toasted

1 Roll 2 pepper strips into each prosciutto slice; set aside. In medium bowl, mash avocado. Stir in mayonnaise, lemon juice, salt and pepper.

2 In 10-inch nonstick skillet, heat 1 tablespoon of the vegetable oil over medium-high heat.

3 Break 1 egg into custard cup; carefully slide into skillet. Repeat with 2 more eggs. Immediately reduce heat to medium-low. Cook 4 minutes, spooning oil over eggs, until film forms over top and whites and yolks are firm, not runny. Repeat with remaining 1 tablespoon oil and 3 eggs. Keep warm.

4 To assemble sandwiches, spread about 2 tablespoons avocado mixture onto half of each waffle. Top each with a prosciutto roll, a fried egg and remaining waffle half. Serve immediately.

1 Sandwich Calories 470; Total Fat 31g (Saturated Fat 7g, Trans Fat 0g); Cholesterol 230mg; Sodium 870mg; Total Carbohydrate 34g (Dietary Fiber 3g); Protein 15g **Exchanges:** 2 Starch, ½ Lean Meat, 1 Medium-Fat Meat, 4½ Fat **Carbohydrate Choices:** 2

Kitchen Secret: You can use 12 (4-inch) square waffles instead of 6 round waffles. Add a splash of red pepper sauce over the top of these sandwiches for a wake-up surprise.

Kitchen Secret: To toast waffles, place in large-slice toaster or heat oven to 350°F. Place ovenproof cooling rack on large rimmed baking sheet. Place waffles on rack. Bake 3 to 4 minutes or until toasted.

Save Time: Prep these deluxe breakfast sandwiches so they can be made-to-order as your family awakes. Make the avocado spread and pepper-prosciutto rolls up to 12 hours before serving. Store separately in airtight container in refrigerator. Waffles can be made and toasted up to 2 hours before serving. Cook eggs to order and assemble sandwiches as eggs are cooking.

CHICKEN-STUFFED WAFFLES

PREP TIME: 40 minutes | START TO FINISH: 40 minutes | Makes 6 waffles

2 cups Original Bisquick mix

1 cup chicken broth

4 tablespoons butter, melted

1 teaspoon ground red pepper (cayenne)

4 green onions, thinly sliced on the bias, green and white parts separated

1 egg

1½ cups finely chopped cooked chicken

1 Brush waffle maker with oil or spray with cooking spray. Heat waffle maker.

2 In large bowl, mix Original Bisquick mix, broth, 2 tablespoons of the melted butter, the red pepper, green onion whites and egg. In small bowl, mix remaining 2 tablespoons melted butter and the chicken.

3 Pour ½ cup of the batter onto center of hot waffle maker. Sprinkle with ¼ cup of the chicken mixture. Close lid of waffle maker. Bake 3 to 4 minutes or until steaming stops. Carefully remove waffle. Repeat with remaining batter and chicken.

4 Top waffles with green onion greens.

1 Waffle Calories 300; Total Fat 14g (Saturated Fat 7g, Trans Fat 0g); Cholesterol 80mg; Sodium 620mg; Total Carbohydrate 29g (Dietary Fiber 1g); Protein 14g **Exchanges:** 2 Starch, 1 Very Lean Meat, 2½ Fat **Carbohydrate Choices:** 2

Kitchen Secret: Don't like spicy flavors? Leave out the ground red pepper—these waffles still have plenty of flavor.

Save Time: Dinner on the run? You can make the waffles the day before and pop them in the toaster before you dash out the door! (Skip the green onions and syrup.) Cool the cooked waffles on a cooling rack, then transfer to a plate and cover with plastic wrap. Store in the refrigerator.

Kitchen Secret: Serve these Southern-style waffles with warmed maple syrup, if desired.

BACON, CORN AND HASH BROWN WAFFLES

PREP TIME: 30 minutes | START TO FINISH: 30 minutes | Makes 5 waffles

3 eggs
6 cups frozen shredded hash brown potatoes (from 30-oz bag), thawed
1 cup shredded cheddar cheese
½ cup Original Bisquick mix
½ cup chopped crisply cooked bacon
½ cup frozen corn, thawed
¼ cup milk
2 tablespoons finely chopped green onion
½ teaspoon salt
¾ cup chive-and-onion sour cream potato topper

1 Brush waffle maker with vegetable oil or spray with cooking spray. Heat waffle maker.

2 In large bowl, beat eggs with whisk until fluffy. Stir in potatoes, cheese, Original Bisquick mix, bacon, corn, milk, green onion and salt until well mixed.

3 Scoop about 1 cup of waffle mixture onto center of hot waffle maker. Spread slightly; close lid of waffle maker.

4 Bake 2 to 3 minutes or until waffle is golden brown. Carefully remove waffle to cooling rack; repeat with remaining batter. Serve topped with a dollop of chive-and-onion sour cream potato topper.

1 Waffle Calories 530; Total Fat 21g (Saturated Fat 11g, Trans Fat 0g); Cholesterol 165mg; Sodium 870mg; Total Carbohydrate 66g (Dietary Fiber 6g); Protein 19g **Exchanges:** 3½ Starch, 1 Other Carbohydrate, ½ Medium-Fat Meat, ½ High-Fat Meat, 2½ Fat **Carbohydrate Choices:** 4½

Save Time: To quickly thaw frozen hash brown potatoes, place in large microwavable bowl. Microwave on High for 3 to 4 minutes, stirring after each minute and breaking up large pieces with a spoon.

Kitchen Secret: Serve waffles topped with extra slices of crisply cooked and crumbled bacon and sliced green onion. Or top with your favorite salsa or maple syrup.

MEXICAN WAFFLE BOWLS

PREP TIME: 35 minutes | **START TO FINISH:** 35 minutes | Makes 5 waffle bowls

1 Heat oven to 350°F. Spray outsides of 5 (6-oz) custard cups with cooking spray. Place upside down on 15 × 10 × 1-inch pan.

2 Brush waffle maker with vegetable oil or spray with cooking spray. Heat waffle maker.

3 In medium bowl, stir all Waffle Bowl ingredients until blended. Pour about ⅓ cup onto center of hot waffle maker. Close lid of waffle maker.

4 Bake about 1½ minutes or until waffle is golden brown. Carefully remove waffle to cooling rack; repeat with remaining batter. Let cool 1 to 2 minutes.

5 Gently roll waffle with rolling pin to flatten. Form flattened waffle over outside of custard cup, pressing lightly to shape. Repeat with remaining batter to make 4 more waffle bowls.

6 Bake 10 to 14 minutes or until waffles are almost dry to touch. Let stand 1 minute. Carefully remove from custard cups and place waffle bowls right side up on cooling rack.

7 Spoon ½ cup rice and beans and ½ cup lettuce into each warm or cool waffle bowl. Top each with 1 tablespoon corn, cheese and pico de gallo. Serve immediately.

WAFFLE BOWLS
- 1 cup Original Bisquick mix
- ½ cup milk
- 2 tablespoons fresh pico de gallo
- 2 tablespoons finely shredded cheddar cheese
- 1 tablespoon vegetable oil
- 1 egg white

FILLING
- 2½ cups prepared seasoned rice and beans (from 7-oz box)
- 2½ cups shredded lettuce
- ⅔ cup hot cooked corn
- 5 tablespoons shredded cheddar cheese
- 5 tablespoons fresh pico de gallo

1 Waffle Bowl Calories 350; Total Fat 10g (Saturated Fat 3.5g, Trans Fat 0g); Cholesterol 10mg; Sodium 930mg; Total Carbohydrate 55g (Dietary Fiber 2g); Protein 10g **Exchanges:** 2 Starch, ½ Vegetable, ½ High-Fat Meat **Carbohydrate Choices:** 3½

Kitchen Secret: If you don't have the prepared rice and bean mix on hand, use your favorite rice and bean recipe. Add other ingredients as you like, such as chopped tomatoes and avocado. For a kick, sprinkle bowls with a little chili powder—yum!

Kitchen Secret: No custard cups? No problem! Crumple 15-inch sheets of aluminum foil into 3-inch balls. Form waffle bowls around balls.

Save Time: To make ahead, prepare Waffle Bowls as directed. After cooling 10 minutes, carefully stack bowls between sheets of waxed paper. Place in airtight container. Freeze. Reheat waffle bowls on ovenproof cooling rack placed on cookie sheet in 350°F oven 3 to 5 minutes.

LET'S MAKE BRUNCH

SAVORY CHEESECAKE BRUNCH BOARD

PREP TIME: 15 minutes | **START TO FINISH:** 1 hour 30 minutes | Makes 18 wedges

¾ cup milk

½ cup Original Bisquick mix

½ teaspoon salt

¼ teaspoon pepper

¼ teaspoon ground red pepper (cayenne)

2 eggs

2 packages (8 oz each) cream cheese, cut into 1-inch pieces and softened

1 cup shredded Swiss cheese (4 oz)

¼ cup shredded Parmesan cheese (1 oz)

¼ cup sliced green onions

1 Heat oven to 350°F. Spray 8-inch square (2-quart) baking dish with cooking spray.

2 Place milk, Original Bisquick mix, salt, pepper, red pepper and eggs in blender. Cover and blend on high speed 15 seconds. Add cream cheese; cover and blend 2 minutes longer. Add cheeses and green onions. Pulse just until combined. Pour into baking dish.

3 Bake 40 to 45 minutes or until knife inserted in center comes out clean. Cool 30 minutes. Serve warm or at room temperature. Cut into 3 rows by 3 rows; cut each square diagonally into 2 wedges.

1 Wedge Calories 150; Total Fat 12g (Saturated Fat 7g, Trans Fat 0g); Cholesterol 55mg; Sodium 220mg; Total Carbohydrate 5g (Dietary Fiber 0g); Protein 5g **Exchanges:** ½ Other Carbohydrate, ½ High-Fat Meat, 1½ Fat **Carbohydrate Choices:** ½

Kitchen Secret: Build a board by arranging cheesecake wedges on large wooden board. Arrange assorted fruit, veggies, nuts, olives and deli meats around board. Serve with crackers or baguette slices.

Kitchen Secret: Top wedges of cheesecake with chopped parsley and small dollops of marinara, olive tapenade or pesto.

GLUTEN-FREE
CAPRESE MINI DUTCH BABIES

PREP TIME: 20 minutes | **START TO FINISH:** 40 minutes | Makes 12 Dutch Babies

½ cup water

3 tablespoons butter

¾ cup Bisquick Gluten Free mix

3 tablespoons chopped julienne-cut sun-dried tomatoes with herbs (from 8.5-oz jar)

2 tablespoons chopped fresh basil leaves

¼ teaspoon salt

3 eggs

4 oz fresh mozzarella, cut into ½-inch cubes (from 8-oz package)

1 Heat oven to 400°F. Generously spray 12 regular-size muffin cups with cooking spray.

2 In 2-quart saucepan, heat water and butter to boiling. Add Bisquick Gluten Free mix, sun-dried tomatoes, 1½ tablespoons of the basil and the salt. Vigorously stir over low heat about 1 minute or until mixture holds together. Remove from heat.

3 With a spoon, beat in eggs, one at a time, beating until smooth and glossy after each addition. Spoon about 2 tablespoons batter into bottom of each muffin cup.

4 Bake 15 to 18 minutes or until puffed and dry in the center. With back of measuring tablespoon, lightly press top of each cup to create a well. Divide mozzarella among cups. Bake 1 to 2 minutes or until cheese softens and begins to melt; sprinkle with remaining basil.

1 Dutch Baby Calories 100; Total Fat 6g (Saturated Fat 3.5g, Trans Fat 0g); Cholesterol 60mg; Sodium 210mg; Total Carbohydrate 8g (Dietary Fiber 0g); Protein 4g **Exchanges:** ½ Other Carbohydrate, ½ Medium-Fat Meat, ½ Fat **Carbohydrate Choices:** ½

Kitchen Secret: Fresh mozzarella cheese is a semisoft cheese that has a high moisture content, so it melts quickly, which makes it perfect for this recipe. Look for it in the deli section of the grocery store. It is available in both balls and logs.

Kitchen Secret: Rich-flavored, dense sun-dried tomatoes like the ones we use in this recipe come dry or packed in oil. We recommend patting them dry with paper towels after chopping to remove the excess oil. Sun-dried tomatoes may be found in several places in the grocery store. Look for them with the tomato products or near pickles and olives. You can always chop more and sprinkle on top after baking, if you like.

LOADED DOUBLE-BACON BREAKFAST BISCUITS

PREP TIME: 20 minutes | START TO FINISH: 40 minutes | Makes 12 biscuits

2 cups Original Bisquick mix

1½ cups shredded sharp cheddar cheese (6 oz)

½ cup chopped cooked bacon (6 slices)

½ cup milk

⅓ cup sliced green onions

¼ cup sour cream

¼ teaspoon garlic powder

3 oz Canadian bacon slices, cut into ½-inch pieces (from 6-oz package)

2 tablespoons butter, melted

1 Heat oven to 425°F. Line large cookie sheet with cooking parchment paper.

2 In large bowl, stir all ingredients except butter until soft dough forms. Drop dough by 12 rounded spoonfuls (about ¼ cup each) onto cookie sheet.

3 Bake 13 to 16 minutes or until golden brown.

4 Brush warm biscuits with melted butter; serve warm.

1 Biscuit Calories 200; Total Fat 13g (Saturated Fat 7g, Trans Fat 0g); Cholesterol 30mg; Sodium 510mg; Total Carbohydrate 13g (Dietary Fiber 0g); Protein 8g **Exchanges:** 1 Starch, ½ High-Fat Meat, 1½ Fat **Carbohydrate Choices:** 1

Kitchen Secret: Enjoy these delicious biscuits on the go by splitting them and filling with a fried egg and slice of cheese.

Save Time: You can store biscuits covered in the refrigerator for a few days. To reheat, microwave an uncovered biscuit on Medium (50%) 20 to 30 seconds or until warm.

PERSONAL CANADIAN BACON BREAKFAST PIZZAS

PREP TIME: 30 minutes | **START TO FINISH:** 45 minutes | Makes 4 pizzas

1 Heat oven to 450°F. Spray large cookie sheet with cooking spray.

2 In medium bowl, mix Crust ingredients until soft dough forms. Divide dough into 4 portions; press each onto cookie sheet to form 6-inch round circles, forming ½-inch ridge around each.

3 In small bowl, beat eggs and 2 tablespoons water. In 8- to 10-inch nonstick skillet, heat butter over medium heat. Add eggs to skillet; cook over medium heat, stirring occasionally, until eggs are set but moist. Remove from heat.

4 Carefully spread 2 tablespoons cream cheese spread on each of the crusts to within ¼ inch of edge. Top with scrambled eggs, Canadian bacon, bell pepper and cheddar cheese.

5 Bake 11 to 13 minutes or until crusts are golden brown and cheese is melted.

1 Pizza Calories 530; Total Fat 37g (Saturated Fat 17g, Trans Fat 0.5g); Cholesterol 210mg; Sodium 1,080mg; Total Carbohydrate 30g (Dietary Fiber 0g); Protein 19g **Exchanges:** 1 Starch, 1 Other Carbohydrate, 2 Medium-Fat Meat, 5½ Fat **Carbohydrate Choices:** 2

Kitchen Secret: Prefer fried eggs? Omit the scrambled eggs, and top each pizza with a fried egg after baking.

Kitchen Secret: Sprinkle pizzas with chopped fresh chives or thinly sliced green onion, if you like.

Save Time: We love Canadian bacon for quick meals because you don't have to cook it first like you do with regular bacon. If you don't have any on hand, you can also use cut-up leftover cooked ham.

CRUST
1½ cups Original Bisquick mix
⅓ cup boiling water
2 tablespoons vegetable oil

SCRAMBLED EGGS
3 eggs
2 tablespoons water
1 tablespoon butter

TOPPINGS
½ cup chive-and-onion cream cheese spread (from 8-oz container)
3 oz Canadian bacon slices, cut into ½-inch pieces (from 6-oz package)
2 tablespoons chopped green bell pepper
¾ cup shredded cheddar cheese (3 oz)

SOUTHWESTERN SCRAMBLE BISCUIT CUPS

PREP TIME: 25 minutes | **START TO FINISH:** 40 minutes | Makes 6 servings (2 biscuit cups each)

1 Heat oven to 350°F. Spray 12 regular-size muffin cups with cooking spray.

2 In medium bowl, stir all Biscuit Cup ingredients until soft dough forms. Divide dough into 12 equal pieces. Press 1 piece into bottom and up side of each muffin cup.

3 Bake 8 to 10 minutes or until light brown.

4 Meanwhile, in large bowl, beat 5 eggs, ¼ cup milk, the salt and pepper; set aside.

5 In 10-inch nonstick skillet, melt 1 tablespoon butter over medium heat. Cook bell pepper, onion and chile for 3 to 5 minutes, stirring occasionally, until tender. Add egg mixture to vegetables. Cook 1 to 2 minutes, stirring occasionally, until eggs are loosely set. Gently fold in cheese.

6 Remove biscuit cups from oven. Using back of spoon, press puffed crust into cup to make deep indentation. Spoon egg mixture into cups.

7 Bake 10 to 15 minutes or just until eggs are set. To remove from pan, run thin knife around biscuit cup and lift out.

BISCUIT CUPS
- 2 cups Original Bisquick mix
- ¼ cup milk
- ¼ cup butter, melted
- 1 tablespoon chili powder
- 1 egg

SCRAMBLE
- 5 eggs
- ¼ cup milk
- ½ teaspoon salt
- ¼ teaspoon pepper
- 1 tablespoon butter
- ¼ cup chopped red bell pepper
- ¼ cup chopped onion
- 1 jalapeño chile, seeded, finely chopped
- 1 cup shredded pepper Jack cheese (4 oz)

1 Serving Calories 400; Total Fat 25g (Saturated Fat 12g, Trans Fat 2g); Cholesterol 255mg; Sodium 980mg; Total Carbohydrate 30g (Dietary Fiber 2g); Protein 14g **Exchanges:** 1½ Starch, ½ Low-Fat Milk, 1 Medium-Fat Meat, 3½ Fat **Carbohydrate Choices:** 2

Kitchen Secret: Wear rubber gloves when seeding and chopping jalapeños to protect your skin from irritation.

Kitchen Secret: Serve these biscuit cups with a dollop of sour cream and salsa.

PEACHY CINNAMON STREUSEL CUPS

PREP TIME: 30 minutes | START TO FINISH: 55 minutes | Makes 12 cups

FILLING

4 oz (half of 8-oz package) cream cheese, softened

3 tablespoons powdered sugar

½ cup finely chopped canned peaches in juice (from 15-oz can), drained on paper towel (reserve 1 tablespoon juice)

MUFFINS

2 cups Original Bisquick mix

¼ cup milk

3 tablespoons firmly packed brown sugar

3 tablespoons butter, softened

1 egg

CRUMB TOPPING

⅓ cup Original Bisquick mix

3 tablespoons firmly packed brown sugar

½ teaspoon ground cinnamon

2 tablespoons cold butter

ICING

½ cup powdered sugar

1 Heat oven to 350°F. Spray 12 regular-size muffin cups with cooking spray.

2 In small bowl, mix cream cheese and the 3 tablespoons powdered sugar until smooth; set aside.

3 In medium bowl, stir together Muffin ingredients until soft dough forms. Divide dough evenly in muffin cups (about 1 generous tablespoon). Spread dough into bottom and up sides of each muffin cup, making a well in the center.

4 In another small bowl, using fork or pastry blender, mix Crumb Topping ingredients until mixture looks like coarse crumbs; set aside.

5 In each cup, spoon 2 teaspoons of cream cheese mixture and scant 1 tablespoon of the peaches; sprinkle evenly with Crumb Topping.

6 Bake 16 to 18 minutes or until edges are light golden brown. Let stand 10 minutes; remove from pan to cooling rack.

7 In small bowl, stir ½ cup powdered sugar and reserved peach syrup until smooth and of drizzling consistency. Drizzle over warm streusel cups. Serve warm. Refrigerate any remaining streusel cups.

1 Cup Calories 230; Total Fat 10g (Saturated Fat 6g, Trans Fat 0g); Cholesterol 40mg; Sodium 300mg; Total Carbohydrate 32g (Dietary Fiber 0g); Protein 3g **Exchanges:** 1 Starch, 1 Other Carbohydrate, 2 Fat **Carbohydrate Choices:** 2

Kitchen Secret: Try canned apricots or pears in place of the peaches.

Save Time: These delicious breakfast pastries can be covered and refrigerated. To reheat, place 1 cup on microwavable plate. Microwave uncovered on High 15 to 30 seconds or until warm.

BAKING BREAKFAST TOGETHER

What a sense of joy and accomplishment your kids will get when they've helped you make breakfast. It's quality time together as well as an opportunity for learning. Make some memories you both can share by baking breakfast together!

Baking Together Tips

Pick an Easy Recipe Select a recipe that has jobs that are appropriate for the age of your helpers. For little ones, simple recipes with a few steps can't miss—dumping ingredients into the bowl or stirring are jobs for them. Older kids can measure, chop and cook.

Read Together Read the recipe together! It's a great habit to get into when cooking, and they can learn new words as well.

Primp Up Tie back long hair, wash hands and sport an apron (not only practical, they look great, too!).

Pull and Prep The younger the kids, the shorter their attention span, so for little chefs, have the ingredients already pulled from the cupboard and prepped. For older kids, allow them to help with this step.

Allow Extra Time It will take longer to make it together than it would if you did it yourself—just plan on it. Having this expectation can make it a lot less stressful! Enjoy the time you have together, even if it goes differently than you planned.

Mess Happens No doubt, spills will happen. Be prepared for them by covering your work area with old newspapers, oil cloth or even a colorful tablecloth from the dollar store.

Supporting Role Have a side dish or two on standby to help round out the meal. Already prepared cut-up fresh fruit and cooked bacon or breakfast sausage means breakfast can be served up as soon as your recipe is finished.

A Dash of Fun

Adding a little fun to your time together will make memories for both you and your mini chefs!

Turn Up the Tunes Play some upbeat, lively music that you both can hum along to . . . or sing into your spoon handles!

Plan for Tasting Who doesn't want to taste their creations? Let your pint-size bakers try a bite of your creation when it's finished.

Artistic Ability Allow your kids to garnish it their way. For pancakes or waffles, have some chocolate and caramel ice-cream toppings and whipped cream in an aerosol can for your budding kitchen Picassos to use. Tiny bowls of toppings or shakers of sprinkles on a cookie sheet with sides will allow them to create a masterpiece while keeping them contained.

Snap Away Don't forget to take pics of the chefs *and* the creations! (And if you want to quickly brush a little Bisquick on their nose before the picture—you have our permission.)

EASY BANANA BREAD COFFEE CAKE

PREP TIME: 15 minutes | **START TO FINISH:** 1 hour 10 minutes | Makes 12 servings

COFFEE CAKE

2 to 3	large ripe bananas, mashed (about 1⅓ cups)
⅔	cup granulated sugar
¼	cup milk
3	tablespoons vegetable oil
1	teaspoon ground cinnamon
3	eggs
2⅔	cups Original Bisquick mix
¾	cup chopped walnuts or pecans
1	large banana, sliced

STREUSEL

1	cup Original Bisquick mix
½	cup chopped walnuts or pecans
½	cup packed brown sugar
6	tablespoons butter, cut into small pieces

1 Heat oven to 350°F. Spray 13×9-inch pan with cooking spray.

2 In large bowl, stir mashed bananas, granulated sugar, milk, oil, cinnamon and eggs. Stir in 2⅔ cups Original Bisquick mix and ¾ cup walnuts. Fold in sliced banana. Pour mixture into pan.

3 In medium bowl, mix Streusel ingredients except butter. Cut in butter with pastry blender or fork until crumbly. Sprinkle over mixture in pan.

4 Bake 30 to 36 minutes or until knife inserted in center comes out clean. Let stand 15 minutes.

5 Cut into 4 rows by 3 rows.

1 Serving Calories 460; Total Fat 24g (Saturated Fat 7g, Trans Fat 1g); Cholesterol 60mg; Sodium 520mg; Total Carbohydrate 54g (Dietary Fiber 2g); Protein 6g **Exchanges:** 2 Starch, 1½ Other Carbohydrate, 4½ Fat **Carbohydrate Choices:** 3½

Save Time: This recipe takes half the time to bake than traditional banana bread takes. Plus, you get to have an entire square (not just a slice) and streusel!

Save Time: You can prepare this coffee cake the night before to give you a jump on breakfast the next day. Prepare it through step 2; cover and refrigerate up to 12 hours. Then uncover and bake as directed in step 3.

Kitchen Secret: You can store any remaining coffee cake covered up to 3 days.

Kitchen Secret: It's not pancakes, but this banana coffee cake is delicious served warm with maple syrup.

CHOCOLATE-HAZELNUT CINNAMON ROLLS

PREP TIME: 20 minutes | START TO FINISH: 45 minutes | Makes 8 rolls

ROLLS

- ¼ cup granulated sugar
- 1 teaspoon ground cinnamon
- 2¾ cups Original Bisquick mix
- ¼ cup milk
- 2 eggs
- 2 tablespoons butter, melted
- ½ cup chopped hazelnuts

TOPPING

- ½ cup powdered sugar
- 2 teaspoons milk
- 2 tablespoons hazelnut spread with cocoa

1 Heat oven to 375°F. Spray 9-inch round cake pan with cooking spray.

2 In small bowl, stir together granulated sugar and cinnamon; reserve 2 tablespoons. In large bowl, stir Original Bisquick mix, remaining sugar-cinnamon mixture, milk and eggs until soft dough forms.

3 Place dough on surface generously sprinkled with Bisquick mix; knead 10 times. Roll dough into 16 × 12-inch rectangle. Brush with butter to within ½ inch from edges; sprinkle evenly with reserved sugar mixture. Sprinkle with hazelnuts. Roll up tightly beginning on short side; seal well by pinching edge of dough. Cut into eight 1½-inch slices; place slices cut side down in pan.

4 Bake 18 to 20 minutes or until light brown. Cool 5 minutes; remove from pan.

5 In small bowl, combine Topping ingredients except hazelnut spread. In small microwavable bowl, heat spread on High for 30 seconds. Drizzle rolls with Topping and then hazelnut spread. Serve warm.

1 Roll Calories 340; Total Fat 13g (Saturated Fat 4g, Trans Fat 0g); Cholesterol 55mg; Sodium 440mg; Total Carbohydrate 48g (Dietary Fiber 2g); Protein 6g **Exchanges:** 1½ Starch, 1½ Other Carbohydrate, ½ High-Fat Meat, 1½ Fat **Carbohydrate Choices:** 3

Kitchen Secret: The hazelnut spread is thick even after heating, so we recommend spooning into a small, resealable plastic bag. Make a tiny cut at one corner and pipe the spread over the rolls. You can also drizzle it with a spoon, but you will get more uneven distribution over the glazed rolls.

Kitchen Secret: If the dough seems a little sticky, gradually mix in enough Bisquick mix, 1 tablespoon at a time, until dough is easy enough to handle.

Kitchen Secret: Hazelnut lovers may want to top these rolls with additional chopped hazelnuts.

MONKEY BREAD

PREP TIME: 20 minutes | **START TO FINISH:** 1 hour 5 minutes | Makes 12 servings

1 Heat oven to 350°F. Spray 12-cup fluted tube cake pan with cooking spray.

2 In large bowl, stir Original Bisquick mix, ¼ cup butter, the milk, 2 tablespoons granulated sugar, vanilla and eggs until soft dough forms. Divide dough into 24 pieces. With greased hands, roll dough into balls.

3 In small bowl, mix ¼ cup granulated sugar and the cinnamon. Roll each dough ball in sugar mixture; place balls randomly in pan. Sprinkle with any remaining sugar mixture.

4 In 2-quart saucepan, melt 1 cup butter. Stir in brown sugar; heat to boiling over medium heat, stirring constantly. Boil 2 minutes; remove from heat. Pour caramel mixture over dough balls in pan.

5 Bake 22 to 28 minutes or until lightly browned on top. Cool 3 to 5 minutes.

6 Place heatproof serving plate upside down over pan; turn plate and pan over. Remove pan; cool 10 minutes. Serve warm.

3	cups Original Bisquick mix
¼	cup butter, melted
¼	cup milk
2	tablespoons granulated sugar
1	teaspoon vanilla
3	eggs
¼	cup granulated sugar
½	teaspoon ground cinnamon
1	cup butter
¾	cup packed brown sugar

1 Serving Calories 380; Total Fat 22g (Saturated Fat 12g, Trans Fat 2g); Cholesterol 100mg; Sodium 510mg; Total Carbohydrate 40g (Dietary Fiber 0g); Protein 4g **Exchanges:** 2 Starch, ½ Other Carbohydrate, 4 Fat **Carbohydrate Choices:** 2½

Kitchen Secret: Brown sugar is always measured firmly packed into the measuring cup.

Kitchen Secret: If you are a nut lover, add ½ cup coarsely chopped pecans to the brown sugar mixture after cooking 2 minutes.

LEMON RASPBERRY BRUNCH CAKE

PREP TIME: 20 minutes | **START TO FINISH:** 1 hour 20 minutes | Makes 12 servings

1 Heat oven to 350°F. Spray 13×9-inch pan with cooking spray.

2 In large bowl, beat all Cake ingredients except raspberries with electric mixer on low speed 30 seconds. Beat on medium speed about 2 minutes or until well blended. Pour batter evenly in pan. Top with raspberries.

3 In medium bowl, stir all Topping ingredients until well mixed. Evenly sprinkle over batter.

4 Bake 30 to 35 minutes or until toothpick inserted in center comes out clean. Cool 30 minutes before serving. Cut into 4 rows by 3 rows.

1 Serving Calories 300; Total Fat 14g (Saturated Fat 6g, Trans Fat 0g); Cholesterol 45mg; Sodium 450mg; Total Carbohydrate 38g (Dietary Fiber 2g); Protein 5g **Exchanges:** 1½ Starch, 1 Other Carbohydrate, 2½ Fat **Carbohydrate Choices:** 2½

Kitchen Secret: For a more decadent cake, serve with a dollop of sweetened whipped cream and sprinkle with grated lemon zest.

Save Time: You can grate lemon zest, or any citrus, and freeze in a small freezer container for an on-hand ingredient.

CAKE

- 3 cups Original Bisquick mix
- ¾ cup milk
- ½ cup sugar
- ¼ cup butter, softened
- 1 tablespoon grated lemon zest
- 1 teaspoon vanilla
- 2 eggs
- 2 cups fresh raspberries

TOPPING

- ⅔ cup sliced almonds
- ⅓ cup sugar
- ¼ cup Original Bisquick mix
- 2 tablespoons butter, melted

PUMPKIN STREUSEL SCONES

PREP TIME: 25 minutes | **START TO FINISH:** 45 minutes | Makes 8 scones

STREUSEL TOPPING

- 3 tablespoons Original Bisquick mix
- 3 tablespoons packed brown sugar
- 2 tablespoons chopped pecans
- ¼ teaspoon pumpkin pie spice
- 2 tablespoons cold butter

SCONES

- 2½ cups Original Bisquick mix
- ⅓ cup packed brown sugar
- ½ teaspoon pumpkin pie spice
- 2 tablespoons cold butter
- ½ cup (from 15-oz can) canned pumpkin (not pumpkin pie mix)
- ¼ cup heavy whipping cream
- 1 egg, beaten

1 Heat oven to 400°F. Spray cookie sheet with cooking spray.

2 In medium bowl, mix all Streusel Topping ingredients except butter. Cut in 2 tablespoons butter, using pastry blender or fork, until mixture is crumbly; set aside.

3 In large bowl, mix 2½ cups Original Bisquick mix, ⅓ cup brown sugar and ½ teaspoon pumpkin pie spice until blended. Cut in 2 tablespoons butter, using pastry blender or fork, until mixture looks like coarse crumbs. In small bowl, mix pumpkin, whipping cream and egg; stir into Bisquick mixture just until combined.

4 Place dough on surface lightly sprinkled with Bisquick mix; knead 6 or 7 times. Place dough in center of cookie sheet. Roll or pat dough into 8-inch round. Cut into 8 wedges with sharp knife, dipping knife in Bisquick mix as necessary. Do not separate into wedges. Sprinkle top of scones with Streusel Topping, lightly patting into dough.

5 Bake 15 to 20 minutes or until light golden brown. Carefully cut into wedges and immediately remove from cookie sheet to cooling rack. Serve warm.

1 Scone Calories 310; Total Fat 13g (Saturated Fat 6g, Trans Fat 0g); Cholesterol 45mg; Sodium 450mg; Total Carbohydrate 44g (Dietary Fiber 1g); Protein 4g **Exchanges:** 1½ Starch, 1½ Other Carbohydrate, 2½ Fat **Carbohydrate Choices:** 3

Kitchen Secret: For a lovely final touch, glaze scones by stirring together ½ cup powdered sugar and 1 tablespoon milk. Drizzle over warm scones.

Kitchen Secret: For smaller scones, use large baking sheet. Divide dough in half after kneading and shape each half into a ball. Pat each into 6-inch circle. Place on baking sheet about 2 inches apart. Cut each wedge into 6 scones, but do not separate. Bake 13 to 15 minutes.

EASY BLUEBERRY MUFFINS

PREP TIME: 10 minutes | **START TO FINISH:** 30 minutes | Makes 12 muffins

2 cups Original Bisquick mix

⅔ cup milk

⅓ cup sugar

2 tablespoons vegetable oil

1 egg

¾ cup fresh or frozen (thawed and drained) blueberries

1 Heat oven to 400°F. Place paper baking cup in each of 12 regular-size muffin cups, or spray bottoms only of muffin cups with cooking spray.

2 In medium bowl, stir all ingredients except blueberries just until moistened. Gently stir in blueberries. Divide batter evenly among cups.

3 Bake 13 to 18 minutes or until golden brown. Cool 5 minutes. Remove muffins from pan to cooling rack.

1 Muffin Calories 140; Total Fat 4.5g (Saturated Fat 1g, Trans Fat 0g); Cholesterol 15mg; Sodium 200mg; Total Carbohydrate 22g (Dietary Fiber 0g); Protein 2g **Exchanges:** 1 Starch, ½ Other Carbohydrate, 1 Fat **Carbohydrate Choices:** 1½

Kitchen Secret: Mix just until dry ingredients are moistened, even though there may be lumps remaining. Overmixing causes tunnels and a tougher texture in the muffins.

Kitchen Secret: Stirring in the blueberries at the end will prevent them from breaking up and turning the batter a dull blue or gray color.

GLUTEN-FREE DOUGHNUT HOLES

PREP TIME: 45 minutes | **START TO FINISH:** 45 minutes | Makes 24 doughnut holes

Vegetable oil for deep frying

¼ cup granulated sugar

½ teaspoon ground cinnamon

1¼ cups Bisquick Gluten Free mix

⅓ cup buttermilk

¼ cup packed brown sugar

2 tablespoons butter, melted

¼ teaspoon ground nutmeg

1 egg, beaten

1 In deep fryer or 2-quart saucepan, heat 2 to 3 inches oil to 375°F.

2 In shallow bowl, mix granulated sugar and cinnamon; set aside. In medium bowl, mix remaining ingredients until smooth. Shape dough into 24 (1¼-inch) balls.

3 Carefully drop balls, 5 or 6 at a time, into hot oil. Fry about 1 to 2 minutes or until golden brown on all sides; drain on paper towels. Immediately roll doughnut holes in cinnamon-sugar mixture.

1 Doughnut Hole Calories 60; Total Fat 2g (Saturated Fat 1g, Trans Fat 0g); Cholesterol 10mg; Sodium 85mg; Total Carbohydrate 10g (Dietary Fiber 0g); Protein 0g **Exchanges:** ½ Starch, ½ Fat **Carbohydrate Choices:** ½

Kitchen Secret: If you don't have buttermilk on hand, mix 1 teaspoon white vinegar in ⅓ cup milk. Let stand 5 minutes.

Kitchen Secret: The oil will drop in temperature as soon as the cool batter hits it, so be sure to allow it to come to temperature again before frying your next batch or your doughnut holes will be heavy and greasy tasting.

RASPBERRY PEEK-A-BOOS

PREP TIME: 20 minutes | START TO FINISH: 40 minutes | Makes 12 muffins

1 Heat oven to 400°F. Place paper baking cup in each of 12 regular-size muffin cups, or spray muffin cups with cooking spray.

2 In small bowl, toss raspberries, 2 tablespoons of the granulated sugar, the lemon juice, nutmeg and cinnamon. Set aside.

3 In medium bowl, mix Original Bisquick mix, remaining 2 tablespoons granulated sugar and the butter. Add milk all at once; stir just until moistened.

4 Spread tablespoonful of dough in bottom of each muffin cup. Top each with 1 tablespoon raspberry mixture. Drop slightly less than 1 tablespoonful dough onto berries.

5 Bake 13 to 15 minutes or until golden brown. Cool slightly; remove from muffin pans to cooling rack. Let stand 10 minutes.

6 In small bowl, stir together Glaze ingredients, adding milk 1 tablespoon at a time until of drizzling consistency. Drizzle over muffins.

MUFFINS
- 1 cup fresh raspberries
- 4 tablespoons granulated sugar
- 1 teaspoon lemon juice
- ½ teaspoon ground nutmeg
- ½ teaspoon ground cinnamon
- 2 cups Original Bisquick mix
- ¼ cup butter, softened
- ⅔ cup milk

GLAZE
- 1 cup powdered sugar
- ½ teaspoon vanilla
- Pinch of salt
- 1 to 2 tablespoons milk

1 Muffin Calories 190; Total Fat 7g (Saturated Fat 4g, Trans Fat 0g); Cholesterol 10mg; Sodium 290mg; Total Carbohydrate 28g (Dietary Fiber 0g); Protein 2g **Exchanges:** ½ Starch, 1½ Other Carbohydrate, 1½ Fat **Carbohydrate Choices:** 2

Kitchen Secret: Those lemon-shaped bottles of juice are handy, but they really don't offer great lemon flavor. We prefer to use fresh lemon juice. Taste how it brightens the flavor of these freshly baked muffins!

Kitchen Secret: If your drizzle looks more like a blob, try these tips. Make sure the glaze is thin enough, otherwise it will tend to fall off the spoon rather than form sort of a "line." You can also start drizzling with strokes that begin before you hit the muffin and end after it. That way, any icing blobs aren't on the muffins!

CANADIAN BACON <u>AND</u> MUSHROOM EGG BAKE

PREP TIME: 25 minutes | **START TO FINISH:** 1 hour | Makes 8 servings

1 Heat oven to 350°F. Spray 13×9-inch (3-quart) baking dish with cooking spray.

2 In 12-inch nonstick skillet, heat 2 tablespoons of the oil over medium heat. Cook onion in oil about 2 minutes, stirring occasionally, until tender. Add remaining 1 tablespoon oil, the mushrooms, thyme, salt and pepper. Cook 5 to 7 minutes, stirring occasionally, until mushrooms are tender and browned. Add arugula; cook about 1 minute or until starting to wilt.

3 In large bowl, beat eggs, milk and Original Bisquick mix until mixed well. Stir in onion mixture, Canadian bacon and cheeses; pour into baking dish.

4 Bake 25 to 32 minutes or until edges are golden brown and knife inserted in center comes out clean. Let stand 5 minutes before serving.

1 Serving Calories 270; Total Fat 18g (Saturated Fat 7g, Trans Fat 0g); Cholesterol 215mg; Sodium 600mg; Total Carbohydrate 9g (Dietary Fiber 0g); Protein 18g **Exchanges:** 1 Vegetable, 2½ Medium-Fat Meat, 1 Fat **Carbohydrate Choices:** ½

Kitchen Secret: For an extra-cheesy top, sprinkle with an additional ¼ cup shredded Parmesan cheese before baking.

Save Time: After step 3, cover and refrigerate at least 8 hours but no longer than 24 hours. In step 4, heat oven to 350°F. Increase bake time to 30 to 38 minutes.

3	tablespoons vegetable oil
½	cup chopped onion
1	package (8 oz) sliced baby portabella mushrooms
½	teaspoon dried thyme leaves
¼	teaspoon salt
¼	teaspoon pepper
2	cups packed baby arugula, chopped
8	eggs
¾	cup milk
½	cup Original Bisquick mix
1	package (6 oz) sliced Canadian bacon, cut into ½-inch pieces
1	cup shredded Italian cheese blend (4 oz)
½	cup shredded Parmesan cheese (2 oz)

15-minute prep
8 ingredients or less

CHOCOLATE-COCONUT FRENCH TOAST STRATA

PREP TIME: 15 minutes | START TO FINISH: 1 hour 5 minutes | Makes 8 servings (2 slices each)

16 (1-inch) slices French bread
2 cups original almond milk
½ cup butter, melted
10 eggs
1 cup Original Bisquick mix
1 cup shredded coconut
⅓ cup miniature semisweet chocolate chips

1 Heat oven to 325°F. Spray 13×9-inch (3-quart) baking dish with cooking spray.

2 Arrange 8 bread slices, overlapping slightly, down the length of one side of the baking dish; repeat with remaining bread slices on other side of the dish.

3 In large bowl, beat almond milk, butter and eggs with whisk. Stir in Original Bisquick mix and ¾ cup of the coconut. Slowly pour mixture over the bread slices, using a fork to lift bread slices to make sure all surfaces are coated with the egg mixture. Sprinkle with chocolate chips and the remaining ¼ cup coconut.

4 Bake 45 to 50 minutes or until knife inserted in center comes out clean. Let stand 15 minutes. Serve warm.

1 Serving Calories 560; Total Fat 28g (Saturated Fat 15g, Trans Fat 0g); Cholesterol 265mg; Sodium 830mg; Total Carbohydrate 60g (Dietary Fiber 3g); Protein 18g **Exchanges:** 3 Starch, 1 Other Carbohydrate, 1 High-Fat Meat, 3½ Fat **Carbohydrate Choices:** 4

Kitchen Secret: Serve this unique French toast with warm maple syrup.

Save Time: This strata can be prepared the night before and baked in the morning. Prepare as directed through step 3 except cover and refrigerate. When ready to bake, heat oven as directed and continue with step 4. Check for doneness in several places in the row between the bread slices. Any remaining liquid on top of strata will absorb during the standing time.

EGGS BENEDICT CASSEROLE

PREP TIME: 25 minutes | **START TO FINISH:** 1 hour 5 minutes | Makes 8 servings

CASSEROLE

- 10 eggs, slightly beaten
- 2 cups half-and-half
- ⅓ cup Original Bisquick mix
- ⅓ cup chopped onion
- ½ teaspoon dried thyme leaves
- ½ teaspoon salt
- ¼ teaspoon pepper
- 1 clove garlic, finely chopped
- 6 English muffins, split, each cut in 6 pieces (about 8 cups)
- 1 package (6 oz) sliced Canadian bacon, cut in quarters

TOPPINGS

- 1 package (1.25 oz) hollandaise sauce mix
- 2 tablespoons chopped fresh chives

1 Heat oven to 350°F. Spray 13 × 9-inch (3-quart) glass baking dish with cooking spray.

2 In large bowl, beat eggs, half-and-half, Original Bisquick mix, onion, thyme, salt, pepper and garlic with whisk until well blended. Stir in English muffin pieces and Canadian bacon; mix well. Pour into baking dish.

3 Bake 25 to 30 minutes or until golden brown and knife inserted in center comes out clean. Let stand 10 minutes before serving.

4 Meanwhile, make hollandaise sauce as directed on package. Pour over top of casserole. Sprinkle with chives.

1 Serving Calories 320; Total Fat 15g (Saturated Fat 7g, Trans Fat 0g); Cholesterol 270mg; Sodium 680mg; Total Carbohydrate 28g (Dietary Fiber 2g); Protein 19g **Exchanges:** 2 Starch, 1 Lean Meat, 1 Medium-Fat Meat, 1 Fat **Carbohydrate Choices:** 2

Kitchen Secret: No Canadian bacon? Use chopped cooked ham instead.

Save Time: After preparing through step 2, cover and refrigerate at least 2 hours but no longer than 12 hours. Heat oven to 350°F. Uncover casserole; stir mixture. Continue as directed in step 3, increasing bake time to 30 to 35 minutes.

IMPOSSIBLY EASY BACON, EGG AND TOT BAKE

PREP TIME: 15 minutes | START TO FINISH: 55 minutes | Makes 8 servings

2 cups milk

1 cup Original Bisquick mix

¼ teaspoon pepper

4 eggs

1 lb bacon, crisply cooked and chopped

6 cups potato nuggets frozen potatoes (from 32-oz bag)

1 cup shredded cheddar cheese (4 oz)

1 tablespoon sliced green onion

1 Heat oven to 400°F. Spray 13 × 9-inch (3-quart) baking dish with cooking spray.

2 In large bowl, stir milk, Original Bisquick mix, pepper and eggs until well blended; pour into baking dish. Top with half of the bacon.

3 Place potato nuggets in single layer in 15 × 10 × 1-inch pan. Place both the baking dish and pan in oven. Bake 20 minutes.

4 Place potato nuggets evenly on top of bake; top with cheese and remaining bacon. Bake 10 to 15 minutes longer or until knife inserted in center comes out clean. Let stand 5 minutes before serving.

5 Top with green onion.

1 Serving Calories 460; Total Fat 26g (Saturated Fat 9g, Trans Fat 4g); Cholesterol 130mg; Sodium 1,160mg; Total Carbohydrate 40g (Dietary Fiber 3g); Protein 17g **Exchanges:** ½ Starch, 2 Other Carbohydrate, ½ Vegetable, 1 Medium-Fat Meat, 1 High-Fat Meat, 2½ Fat **Carbohydrate Choices:** 2½

Kitchen Secret: Use 1 pound cooked and drained ground beef in place of the bacon for a twist on this dish!

Save Time: Get dinner on the table pronto by prepping it in advance. Prepare Bisquick bake as directed through step 2. Cover and refrigerate up to 12 hours. Heat oven to 400°F. Uncover, and continue as directed in step 3.

GLUTEN-FREE SHAKSHUKA BRUNCH TART

PREP TIME: 25 minutes | **START TO FINISH:** 55 minutes | Makes 6 servings

1 Heat oven to 375°F. Spray 9½-inch tart pan with removable bottom with cooking spray.

2 In medium bowl, mix Crust ingredients until soft dough forms. Gather into ball. Press firmly and evenly against bottom and up sides of tart pan. Bake 10 minutes.

3 Meanwhile, in medium skillet, heat salsa, tomato paste, cumin and smoked paprika over medium-high heat to boiling; reduce heat. Simmer uncovered 5 minutes or until slightly thickened. Spread hot tomato mixture in crust. With back of spoon, make 6 (2½-inch) deep indentations in tomato mixture in a circle around the edge of the tart; mound the tomato mixture toward the sides and center of the tart.

4 Break eggs, 1 at a time, into custard cup; carefully slide egg into each indentation.

5 Bake an additional 20 to 25 minutes or until egg whites are firm but yolks are still slightly runny.

6 Sprinkle top of tart with feta cheese and parsley. Cut into wedges.

CRUST

1⅓	cups Bisquick Gluten Free mix
½	cup water
⅓	cup butter, melted and cooled
1	teaspoon Italian seasoning

FILLING

1¾	cups mild or medium chunky salsa
2	tablespoons tomato paste (from 6-oz can)
½	teaspoon ground cumin
¼	teaspoon smoked paprika
6	eggs
½	cup crumbled feta cheese (2 oz)
1	tablespoon chopped fresh parsley

1 Serving Calories 340; Total Fat 18g (Saturated Fat 10g, Trans Fat 0.5g); Cholesterol 225mg; Sodium 1,100mg; Total Carbohydrate 33g (Dietary Fiber 2g); Protein 11g **Exchanges:** 1 Starch, 1 Other Carbohydrate, ½ Vegetable, 1 Medium-Fat Meat, 2½ Fat **Carbohydrate Choices:** 2

Kitchen Secret: If you like your egg yolk firmer, bake the tart a little longer.

Kitchen Secret: To keep the eggs from spreading over the top of the tart, make the indentations almost to the bottom of the tart, building up the sides of the indentations with the tomato mixture. Also push the tomato mixture toward the center of the tart as well as the edge.

Kitchen Secret: Shakshuka is a classic Mediterranean dish of eggs cooked in a spicy tomato sauce. We've adapted this popular dish by adding a crust to the bottom for an all-in-one meal.

EASY BACON <u>AND</u> ASPARAGUS EGG CASSEROLE

PREP TIME: 25 minutes | **START TO FINISH:** 1 hour 15 minutes | Makes 12 servings

1 Heat oven to 400°F. Spray 13×9-inch (3-quart) baking dish with cooking spray.

2 In baking dish, mix 1 cup of the bacon, the hash browns, asparagus, tomatoes, ¼ cup of the green onions, 1½ cups of the cheese, the salt, thyme and pepper until well blended. Set aside.

3 In large bowl, beat milk, Original Bisquick mix and eggs with whisk until well blended. Pour evenly over bacon–hash brown mixture in baking dish.

4 Bake 30 to 35 minutes or until knife inserted in center comes out clean. Sprinkle with remaining bacon and ½ cup cheese. Bake 2 to 3 minutes longer or until cheese is melted. Let stand 10 minutes before serving.

5 Sprinkle with remaining ¼ cup green onions.

1 Serving Calories 240; Total Fat 14g (Saturated Fat 6g, Trans Fat 0g); Cholesterol 120mg; Sodium 530mg; Total Carbohydrate 17g (Dietary Fiber 1g); Protein 13g **Exchanges:** 1 Starch, ½ Vegetable, ½ Medium-Fat Meat, ½ High-Fat Meat, 1½ Fat **Carbohydrate Choices:** 1

Save Time: This easy breakfast casserole can be prepared, covered and refrigerated up to 24 hours before baking. Heat oven to 400°F. Uncover and bake as directed in step 4. Increase bake time 5 to 10 minutes.

Kitchen Secret: Serve this easy casserole for brunch or dinner. The leftovers reheat nicely for a quick meal before you head out the door.

Save Time: You can cook the bacon ahead of time and store it in a resealable food-storage bag in your refrigerator or freezer to get a jump on meal preparation. Since the bacon needs to be cut before cooking to retain larger pieces, cook the bacon pieces in a nonstick skillet on medium-high heat, stirring occasionally, until brown and crisp. Drain bacon on paper towels.

12 slices bacon, cut into 1-inch pieces, crisply cooked

2 cups refrigerated hash browns (from 20-oz package)

2 cups ½-inch fresh asparagus pieces

1 cup seeded, chopped plum (Roma) tomatoes (about 2 medium)

½ cup sliced green onions

2 cups shredded cheddar cheese (8 oz)

½ teaspoon salt

¼ teaspoon dried thyme leaves

¼ teaspoon ground black pepper

2 cups milk

1 cup Original Bisquick mix

6 eggs

IMPOSSIBLY EASY BREAKFAST BAKE

PREP TIME: 20 minutes | **START TO FINISH:** 1 hour 10 minutes | Makes 12 servings

2 packages (12 oz each) bulk pork sausage

1 medium bell pepper, chopped (1 cup)

1 medium onion, chopped (½ cup)

3 cups frozen hash brown potatoes

2 cups shredded cheddar cheese (8 oz)

2 cups milk

1 cup Original Bisquick mix

¼ teaspoon pepper

4 eggs

1 Heat oven to 400°F. Spray 13 × 9-inch (3-quart) baking dish with cooking spray.

2 In 10-inch skillet, cook sausage, bell pepper and onion over medium heat, stirring occasionally, until sausage is no longer pink; drain. In baking dish, stir together sausage mixture, hash brown potatoes and 1½ cups of the cheese.

3 In large bowl, stir together milk, Original Bisquick mix, pepper and eggs until blended. Pour into baking dish.

4 Bake 40 to 45 minutes or until knife inserted in center comes out clean. Sprinkle with remaining ½ cup cheese. Bake 1 to 2 minutes longer or just until cheese is melted. Let stand 5 minutes before serving.

1 Serving Calories 300; Total Fat 18g (Saturated Fat 8g, Trans Fat 0g); Cholesterol 115mg; Sodium 490mg; Total Carbohydrate 20g (Dietary Fiber 1g); Protein 15g **Exchanges:** 1½ Starch, 1½ High-Fat Meat, 1 Fat **Carbohydrate Choices:** 1

Kitchen Secret: Make it supreme! Add 1 jar (4.5 oz) sliced mushrooms, drained, with the potatoes and sprinkle with 2 tablespoons chopped green onions or chives just before serving.

Save Time: If you have leftover chopped cooked veggies, feel free to use a cup of them and skip chopping the bell peppers.

Kitchen Secret: If the frozen hash browns are in clumps, use the end of a table knife or a wooden spoon to break up large pieces while the hash browns are still in the bag.

BACON, EGG AND CHEESE BRAID

PREP TIME: 35 minutes | START TO FINISH: 1 hour 5 minutes | Makes 8 servings

6 slices bacon, cut into
   1-inch pieces

6 eggs

¼ teaspoon salt

¼ teaspoon pepper

¼ cup chopped
   green onions

¼ cup chopped red
   bell pepper

2 cups Original
   Bisquick mix

3 oz (from 8-oz package)
   cream cheese, softened

¼ cup cold butter

⅓ cup milk

2 cups shredded Colby–
   Monterey Jack cheese
   (8 oz)

1 Heat oven to 400°F.

2 In 10-inch nonstick skillet, cook bacon until crisp. Remove bacon from skillet to paper towels. Reserve 1 tablespoon bacon drippings in pan.

3 In medium bowl, beat eggs, salt and pepper. Add eggs to skillet; cook over medium-high heat, stirring occasionally, until eggs are set but moist. Remove from heat. Stir in 3 tablespoons of the green onions and the bell pepper until well mixed. Set aside.

4 Place Original Bisquick mix in large bowl. Using pastry blender or fork, cut in cream cheese and butter until crumbly. Stir in milk until dough forms. Place dough on surface sprinkled with Bisquick mix; roll in Bisquick mix to coat. Knead 8 to 10 times.

5 Using rolling pin, roll dough into 12 × 10-inch rectangle. Carefully transfer to large ungreased cookie sheet. Spoon egg mixture in 4-inch strip down center of dough. Top with ½ cup of the bacon and 1 cup of the cheese. With sharp knife, make cuts 1 inch apart on long sides of dough rectangle to within ¼ inch of filling. Fold strips over filling to within ½ inch of center, overlapping strips.

6 Bake 15 to 20 minutes or until golden brown. Sprinkle with remaining bacon and 1 cup cheese. Bake 2 to 3 minutes longer or until cheese is melted.

7 Sprinkle with remaining 1 tablespoon green onion. Let stand 5 minutes before serving.

1 Serving Calories 410; Total Fat 30g (Saturated Fat 15g, Trans Fat 0.5g); Cholesterol 195mg; Sodium 840mg; Total Carbohydrate 20g (Dietary Fiber 0g); Protein 16g **Exchanges:** 1½ Other Carbohydrate, 1 Medium-Fat Meat, 1 High-Fat Meat, 3½ Fat **Carbohydrate Choices:** 1

Save Time: Cold butter gets cut into the Bisquick mix and cream cheese because it will get to a crumbly texture faster and easier than if the butter is softened. You can cut even more time in this step by cutting the butter into small pieces before adding it to the other ingredients.

Kitchen Secret: If the dough sticks to the knife when cutting dough strips, dip knife into Bisquick mix.

IMPOSSIBLY EASY MAPLE SAUSAGE PIE

PREP TIME: 20 minutes | **START TO FINISH:** 1 hour | Makes 6 servings

12 oz bulk maple sausage or raw maple sausage links, casings removed

3 green onions, thinly sliced, green and white parts separated

1 cup Original Bisquick mix

1 cup milk

½ teaspoon salt

3 eggs

1 cup shredded mozzarella cheese (4 oz)

1 tablespoon real maple syrup

1 Heat oven to 375°F. Spray 9-inch glass pie plate with cooking spray.

2 In 10-inch skillet, cook sausage and green onion whites over medium heat 7 to 8 minutes, stirring occasionally, until sausage is no longer pink; drain. Spread in pie plate.

3 In medium bowl, stir Original Bisquick mix, milk, salt and eggs until blended. Stir in cheese. Pour into pie plate.

4 Bake 30 to 35 minutes or until knife inserted in center comes out clean. Let stand 5 minutes before serving.

5 Drizzle with maple syrup; top with green onion greens.

1 Serving Calories 340; Total Fat 20g (Saturated Fat 7g, Trans Fat 0g); Cholesterol 140mg; Sodium 870mg; Total Carbohydrate 21g (Dietary Fiber 0g); Protein 18g **Exchanges:** 1½ Other Carbohydrate, ½ Medium-Fat Meat, 2 High-Fat Meat, ½ Fat **Carbohydrate Choices:** 1½

Save Time: If you need to remove the casings from your sausage, you can do it quickly and easily by slitting up one side with kitchen scissors. Then just open the casing with your fingers, flip over the sausage, and the meat should just drop away from the casing.

Kitchen Secret: Sharp cheddar makes a terrific substitute for the mozzarella in this recipe.

Kitchen Secret: Cut the pie into small squares for a fun brunch-size appetizer option.

SKILLET CHEDDAR BISCUITS AND SAUSAGE GRAVY

PREP TIME: 15 minutes | **START TO FINISH:** 35 minutes | Makes 8 servings

1. Heat oven to 400°F.

2. In medium bowl, stir together Original Bisquick mix and the ½ cup milk; stir until well mixed. Stir in cheese. Set aside.

3. In 10-inch cast iron or ovenproof skillet, melt butter over medium-high heat. Add sausage; cook 5 to 7 minutes, stirring frequently, until no longer pink. Add flour; cook 1 to 2 minutes, stirring frequently, until thickened. Stir in 2 cups milk. Heat to boiling; boil 1 minute. Remove from heat. Drop biscuit dough in 8 large spoonfuls onto hot sausage gravy.

4. Bake 14 to 16 minutes or until biscuits are golden brown.

1 Serving Calories 480; Total Fat 36g (Saturated Fat 15g, Trans Fat 0g); Cholesterol 75mg; Sodium 980mg; Total Carbohydrate 21g (Dietary Fiber 0g); Protein 16g **Exchanges:** ½ Starch, 1 Other Carbohydrate, 2 High-Fat Meat, 4 Fat **Carbohydrate Choices:** 1½

Save Time: This recipe takes the time and effort out of baking biscuits and making gravy separately. You'll also love the time you save cleaning only one pan!

Kitchen Secret: A cast iron skillet works well in this recipe because it looks great and helps the biscuits brown beautifully. But you can use a stainless steel ovenproof skillet if you don't have a cast iron one.

Kitchen Secret: Most Southerners would balk at sprinkling something green on top of this delicacy. But if you absolutely must add a garnish, sliced green onions would be a good choice.

BISCUITS
- 1½ cups Original Bisquick mix
- ½ cup milk
- 1 cup shredded white cheddar cheese (4 oz)

GRAVY
- 2 tablespoons butter
- 1 lb bulk breakfast sausage
- ¼ cup all-purpose flour
- 2 cups milk

EASY APPS
AND BREADS

BLOODY MARY WAFFLE BITES

PREP TIME: 30 minutes | **START TO FINISH:** 30 minutes | Makes 48 appetizers

WAFFLES

- 1 cup Original Bisquick mix
- ½ cup milk
- 1 tablespoon olive oil
- 1 teaspoon Bloody Mary seasoning
- 1 egg
- ¼ cup finely chopped tomato
- ¼ cup finely chopped celery

TOPPING

- ⅓ cup mayonnaise or salad dressing
- 2 teaspoons prepared horseradish
- 1 teaspoon Bloody Mary seasoning

1 Brush waffle maker with vegetable oil or spray with cooking spray. Heat waffle maker.

2 In medium bowl, mix all Waffle ingredients except tomato and celery until well blended. Stir in tomato and celery.

3 Pour about ⅓ cup of batter onto center of hot waffle maker. Close lid of waffle maker.

4 Bake 1 to 2 minutes or until waffle is golden brown. Carefully remove waffle to cooling rack; repeat with remaining batter.

5 In small bowl, mix Topping ingredients until well blended.

6 Cut each waffle into 8 wedges. To toast waffles, heat oven to 350°F. Place ovenproof wire rack on large rimmed baking sheet. Place waffle wedges on rack. Bake 2 to 3 minutes or until crisp.

7 Spoon about ½ teaspoon Topping onto each wedge. Serve warm.

1 Appetizer Calories 25; Total Fat 2g (Saturated Fat 0g, Trans Fat 0g); Cholesterol 0mg; Sodium 40mg; Total Carbohydrate 2g (Dietary Fiber 0g); Protein 0g **Exchanges:** ½ Fat **Carbohydrate Choices:** 0

Kitchen Secret: Bloody Mary seasoning, or rim salt, can be found in many supermarket spice or beverage sections. It may also be found in a well-stocked liquor store. To make your own, stir together 2 tablespoons kosher salt and 1 teaspoon each celery salt, ground cumin, garlic powder, smoked paprika and lemon-pepper seasoning.

Kitchen Secret: Get creative with over-the-top garnishes for these fun appetizers. Load a toothpick with 2 or 3 of any of the following: small pickles, artichoke hearts, cherry tomatoes, cooked bacon, salami, olives, cucumbers or other favorite Bloody Mary garnishes. Place toothpick into top of each waffle wedge.

* 15-minute prep
* 8 ingredients or less
* 30 minutes or less

MINI PESTO APPETIZER PIZZAS

PREP TIME: 15 minutes | **START TO FINISH:** 30 minutes | Makes 12 appetizer pizzas

1½ cups Original Bisquick mix

¼ cup very hot water

⅓ cup prepared basil pesto

3 slices Provolone cheese, each cut into 8 wedges

12 grape tomatoes, each cut into 3 slices

1 Heat oven to 450°F.

2 In medium bowl, stir together Bisquick mix, hot water and 2 tablespoons of the pesto; beat 20 strokes until soft dough forms.

3 Place dough on surface generously sprinkled with Original Bisquick; roll dough into 10×6-inch rectangle. Using 2½-inch round cookie cutter, cut into 8 rounds. Reroll dough and cut 4 more rounds. Place on ungreased cookie sheet. Spread each round with about 1 teaspoon pesto; top each with 2 pieces of cheese and 3 tomato slices.

4 Bake about 6 minutes or until crust is light brown. Serve warm.

1 Appetizer Pizza Calories 200; Total Fat 7g (Saturated Fat 2.5g, Trans Fat 0g); Cholesterol 0mg; Sodium 490mg; Total Carbohydrate 29g (Dietary Fiber 1g); Protein 4g **Exchanges:** ½ Starch, 1½ Fat **Carbohydrate Choices:** 2

Kitchen Secret: You can personalize these pizzas by using pizza sauce instead of the pesto. You can also add mini pepperoni, cooked sausage crumbles or cooked ground beef before topping with cheese. Top with small fresh basil leaves for a simple garnish.

Kitchen Secret: Grape tomatoes are small and sweet like cherry tomatoes but have an oval or oblong shape. You can also use cherry tomatoes in this recipe. Just cut the slices evenly.

CHEESY MEATBALL CUPS

PREP TIME: 15 minutes | **START TO FINISH:** 35 minutes | Makes 24 cups

2 cups Original Bisquick mix

¾ cup shredded Parmesan cheese

½ teaspoon Italian seasoning

¼ teaspoon garlic powder

⅔ cup milk

½ cup tomato pasta sauce

24 frozen fully cooked meatballs

1 Heat oven to 425°F. Spray 24 mini muffin cups with cooking spray.

2 In medium bowl, stir Original Bisquick mix, Parmesan cheese, Italian seasoning and garlic powder. Stir in milk until soft dough forms. Spoon generous 1 tablespoon dough into each muffin cup. With fingers dusted with Bisquick mix, press dough into bottom and up sides of muffin cups. Spoon ½ teaspoon pasta sauce into each cup; top with a meatball.

3 Bake 15 to 20 minutes or until crust is golden brown and center of meatball reaches 165°F. Let stand 2 minutes before removing from pan. Spoon remaining pasta sauce over meatballs.

1 Cup Calories 130; Total Fat 6g (Saturated Fat 2.5g, Trans Fat 0g); Cholesterol 30mg; Sodium 330mg; Total Carbohydrate 11g (Dietary Fiber 0g); Protein 8g **Exchanges:** ½ Starch, 1 Medium-Fat Meat **Carbohydrate Choices:** 1

Kitchen Secret: When buying a tomato pasta sauce, look for one that is slightly thicker and smoother rather than one with chunks of veggies. For something completely different, swap pesto sauce for the tomato pasta sauce. Top each meatball cup with thinly sliced fresh basil.

Kitchen Secret: Cooled Meatball Cups can be frozen in a resealable freezer storage bag. To reheat, place 4 meatball cups on microwavable plate. Cover with waxed paper. Heat on medium (50%) power 2 to 3 minutes or until hot.

CHEESY HERB PULL-APART

PREP TIME: 40 minutes | **START TO FINISH:** 55 minutes | Makes 32 appetizers

1 Heat oven to 400°F. Spray large baking sheet with cooking spray.

2 In small bowl, combine oregano, rosemary and parsley; set aside. In large bowl, stir Original Bisquick mix, milk and egg until soft dough forms. Shape into a ball. If necessary, add 1 teaspoon of milk, 1 teaspoon at a time, to make dough easier to shape.

3 Divide dough into 32 balls. For each appetizer, slightly flatten a dough ball; top with about ¼ teaspoon of the herb mixture and 1 cube of cheese. Wrap dough around cheese and herbs, covering completely; pinch to seal. Repeat with remaining dough balls, herb mixture and cheese cubes.

4 Arrange balls, sealed side down, with sides touching in an oval shape in center of baking sheet.

5 Bake 11 to 13 minutes or until light golden brown.

6 Meanwhile, in small bowl, stir together butter, 3 tablespoons of the Parmesan cheese and the remaining herbs.

7 Spoon and spread the butter mixture over the hot pull-apart. Sprinkle with the remaining 1 tablespoon of Parmesan cheese. Serve immediately with tomato pasta sauce.

2	tablespoons chopped fresh oregano leaves
1½	tablespoons chopped fresh rosemary leaves
1½	tablespoons chopped fresh Italian parsley
3½	cups Original Bisquick mix
½	cup milk
1	egg
12	oz mozzarella cheese, cut into 32 (¾-inch) cubes
3	tablespoons butter, melted
¼	cup grated Parmesan cheese
1	cup tomato pasta or marinara sauce, heated through

1 Appetizer Calories 100; Total Fat 5g (Saturated Fat 2.5g, Trans Fat 0g); Cholesterol 15mg; Sodium 250mg; Total Carbohydrate 11g (Dietary Fiber 0g); Protein 4g **Exchanges:** 1 Other Carbohydrate, ½ Medium-Fat Meat, ½ Fat **Carbohydrate Choices:** 1

Kitchen Secret: Easily transfer the pull-apart to a heatproof decorative serving tray by using two large spatulas.

Kitchen Secret: Arrange the filled dough balls to make a fun shape like a football or a Christmas tree for different holidays and events.

BISCUIT NACHOS

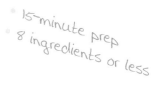

PREP TIME: 15 minutes | START TO FINISH: 40 minutes | Makes 12 servings

1 Heat oven to 400°F.

2 In large bowl, mix Original Bisquick mix and taco seasoning mix; blend well. Stir in milk and 1 cup of the cheese until soft dough forms. Using teaspoon, drop dough, forming 1-inch mounds, onto 2 ungreased baking sheets, about 30 mounds per sheet.

3 Bake sheets one at a time, about 7 minutes each, until biscuits are golden brown. Cool 1 minute; loosen from baking sheets.

4 Line large cookie sheet with foil. Arrange baked biscuits with sides of biscuits touching, randomly and slightly overlapping. Sprinkle 1 cup of the cheese evenly over top of biscuits. Top with beans, olives and pico de gallo. Sprinkle with remaining 1 cup of cheese.

5 Bake about 7 minutes longer or until hot and cheese is melted.

3 cups Original Bisquick mix
1 package (1 oz) taco seasoning mix
1 cup milk
3 cups shredded cheddar cheese
1 can (15 oz) pinto beans, rinsed and drained
1 can (2¼ oz) sliced ripe black olives, drained
1 cup fresh pico de gallo

1 Serving Calories 280; Total Fat 13g (Saturated Fat 6g, Trans Fat 0g); Cholesterol 30mg; Sodium 800mg; Total Carbohydrate 30g (Dietary Fiber 2g); Protein 11g **Exchanges:** 1 Starch, 1 Other Carbohydrate, 1 High-Fat Meat, 1 Fat **Carbohydrate Choices:** 2

Kitchen Secret: To make it party ready, sprinkle nachos with chopped fresh cilantro and serve with sour cream.

Kitchen Secret: If you like a lot of the "topping" part of nachos, arrange biscuits so they are touching, but not overlapping, before topping the biscuits.

SAUSAGE CHEESE BALL APPETIZERS

These savory little bites are simply addictive and never go out of style! The original recipe has been around since the '70s, when no party would have been complete without them. Now we have several delectable variations to choose from. You get to decide which ones to serve or pop in your mouth! Make them the day before, if you like, and bake them up fresh for your gathering. Offer bowls of any of these for dipping:

Cold

Pimiento
cheese spread

Thousand
Island dressing

Blue cheese
dressing

Hot

Cheese dip

Chili sauce

Barbecue sauce

Pasta sauce

SAUSAGE CHEESE BALL APPETIZERS

PREP TIME: 30 minutes   **START TO FINISH:** 55 minutes   Makes about 7 dozen cheese balls

4 cups shredded cheddar cheese (16 oz)

3 cups Original Bisquick mix

1 lb bulk regular or spicy pork sausage

½ cup grated Parmesan cheese

½ cup milk

1½ teaspoons chopped fresh parsley or ½ teaspoon parsley flakes

½ teaspoon dried rosemary leaves, crushed

1 Heat oven to 350°F. Line two 15 × 10 × 1-inch pans with cooking parchment paper or spray with cooking spray.

2 In large bowl, stir together all ingredients using hands or spoon. If mixture seems too stiff, stir in additional milk, 1 tablespoon at a time, just until mixture holds its shape. Shape mixture into 1-inch balls. Place in pans.

3 Bake uncovered 18 to 23 minutes, rotating pans halfway through bake time, or until brown and no longer pink in center. Immediately remove from pan; transfer to serving platter. Serve immediately.

1 Cheese Ball Calories 45; Total Fat 3g (Saturated Fat 1.5g, Trans Fat 0g); Cholesterol 10mg; Sodium 95mg; Total Carbohydrate 2g (Dietary Fiber 0g); Protein 2g **Exchanges:** ½ High-Fat Meat **Carbohydrate Choices:** 0

Kitchen Secret: These savory appetizers are one of Betty Crocker's all-time most-requested recipes. We recommend sprinkling them with chopped parsley and serving with warm chili sauce for dipping. They promise to be a crowd pleaser!

Kitchen Secret: Crushing dried rosemary releases the oils within, intensifying the flavor and aroma.

ITALIAN SAUSAGE CHEESE BALLS

PREP TIME: 30 minutes   **START TO FINISH:** 55 minutes   Makes about 6½ dozen cheese balls

1 Heat oven to 350°F. Line two 15 × 10 × 1-inch baking pans with cooking parchment paper or spray bottom and sides of pans with cooking spray.

2 In large bowl, mix Original Bisquick mix, cheeses, sausage, milk, butter, Italian seasoning and ½ teaspoon of the pepper flakes using hands or spoon. Shape mixture into 1-inch balls. Place in pans.

3 Bake 18 to 23 minutes, rotating pans halfway through bake time, or until brown and no longer pink in center. Immediately remove from pan; transfer to serving platter. Sprinkle with basil.

4 Meanwhile, in 1½-quart saucepan, heat pasta sauce and remaining ½ teaspoon pepper flakes to simmering over medium heat. Reduce heat to medium-low; simmer 5 minutes to combine flavors, stirring frequently. Serve warm cheese balls with sauce.

1 Cheese Ball Calories 60; Total Fat 3.5g (Saturated Fat 1.5g, Trans Fat 0g); Cholesterol 10mg; Sodium 140mg; Total Carbohydrate 4g (Dietary Fiber 0g); Protein 2g **Exchanges:** ½ Starch, ½ Fat **Carbohydrate Choices:** 0

Kitchen Secret: Use slightly damp hands to easily separate and shape the sausage mixture into balls.

Kitchen Secret: If you can't buy bulk Italian sausage, just use 1 pound of uncooked links and remove the casing first.

Kitchen Secret: Garnish these with small sprigs or chopped basil for a party-ready look.

3 cups Original Bisquick mix

2 cups shredded Italian cheese blend (8 oz)

2 cups shredded mozzarella cheese (8 oz)

1 lb bulk Italian pork sausage

½ cup milk

4 tablespoons butter, melted

1 tablespoon Italian seasoning

1 teaspoon crushed red pepper flakes

2 tablespoons finely shredded fresh basil leaves

1 jar (24 oz) tomato basil pasta sauce

BACON CHEESEBURGER BALLS

PREP TIME: 30 minutes | **START TO FINISH:** 55 minutes | Makes about 8 dozen cheese balls

4 cups shredded cheddar cheese (16 oz)

3 cups Original Bisquick mix

½ cup grated Parmesan cheese

½ cup milk

¼ cup dill pickle relish

1 lb ground beef (at least 80% lean)

12 slices bacon, crisply cooked and crumbled

1 Heat oven to 350°F. Spray bottom and sides of two 15 × 10 × 1-inch pans with cooking spray.

2 In large bowl, mix all ingredients using hands or spoon. Shape mixture into 1-inch balls. Place in pans.

3 Bake 20 to 25 minutes, rotating pans halfway through bake time, or until brown and no longer pink in center. Immediately remove from pan; transfer to serving platter. Serve immediately.

1 Cheese Ball Calories 50; Total Fat 3g (Saturated Fat 1.5g, Trans Fat 0g); Cholesterol 10mg; Sodium 105mg; Total Carbohydrate 3g (Dietary Fiber 0g); Protein 2g **Exchanges:** ½ High-Fat Meat **Carbohydrate Choices:** 0

Kitchen Secret: Use ground turkey in place of the ground beef for a twist on a turkey burger.

Save Time: Make as directed through step 2. Cover and refrigerate up to 12 hours. Uncover and bake as directed in step 3.

Kitchen Secret: Serve with mustard and ketchup for dipping.

TURKEY-PARMESAN CHEESE BALLS

PREP TIME: 20 minutes | **START TO FINISH:** 45 minutes | Makes about 4 dozen cheese balls

1 Heat oven to 350°F. Line bottom and sides of 15 × 10 × 1-inch pan with foil. Generously spray foil with cooking spray.

2 In large bowl, mix all ingredients except Parmesan cheese and marinara sauce, using hands or spoon. Shape mixture into 1-inch balls. Place Parmesan cheese in small bowl. Roll balls in Parmesan cheese, pressing to adhere. Place in pan.

3 Bake 18 to 23 minutes or until brown and thoroughly cooked and no longer pink in center. Immediately remove from pan.

4 Serve warm with sauce for dipping.

1 Cheese Ball Calories 60; Total Fat 3.5g (Saturated Fat 2g, Trans Fat 0g); Cholesterol 10mg; Sodium 160mg; Total Carbohydrate 4g (Dietary Fiber 0g); Protein 3g **Exchanges:** ½ Other Carbohydrate, ½ Very Lean Meat, ½ Fat **Carbohydrate Choices:** 0

Kitchen Secret: For the best texture and eating quality, we call for the crispy panko crumbs rather than the regular bread crumbs in this recipe.

Kitchen Secret: You can easily double this recipe for a large crowd. With appetizers this good, they're bound to go fast!

2 cups shredded Italian cheese blend (8 oz)

1½ cups Original Bisquick mix

½ lb bulk mild Italian turkey sausage

½ cup Italian-style crispy panko bread crumbs

½ cup milk

4 tablespoons butter, melted

1 tablespoon Italian seasoning

1 teaspoon dried garlic powder

½ cup grated Parmesan cheese

1 cup marinara sauce, warmed

GLUTEN-FREE JALAPEÑO POPPERETTES

PREP TIME: 20 minutes | START TO FINISH: 35 minutes | Makes 12 popperettes

¼ cup butter, softened

2 tablespoons juice from jar of pickled jalapeños (from 12-oz jar)

1 egg

1 egg yolk

1 cup Gluten Free Bisquick mix

¼ cup shredded pepper Jack cheese (1 oz)

¼ teaspoon garlic powder

¼ teaspoon onion powder

2 oz pepper Jack cheese, cut into 12 cubes

24 pickled jalapeño slices (from 12-oz jar)

1 Heat oven to 400°F. Spray 12 mini muffin cups with cooking spray with flour.

2 In medium bowl, stir butter, jalapeño juice, egg and egg yolk until mixed. Add Gluten Free Bisquick mix, shredded pepper Jack cheese, garlic powder and onion powder; stir until soft dough forms.

3 Wrap dough (about 1 tablespoon) around 1 cheese cube and 1 jalapeño slice; roll to seal. Place balls in muffin cups; top each with a jalapeño slice.

4 Bake 10 to 14 minutes or until light golden brown. Let stand 5 minutes. Serve warm.

1 Popperette Calories 120; Total Fat 7g (Saturated Fat 4g, Trans Fat 0g); Cholesterol 45mg; Sodium 250mg; Total Carbohydrate 10g (Dietary Fiber 0g); Protein 3g **Exchanges:** ½ Starch, 1½ Fat **Carbohydrate Choices:** ½

Kitchen Secret: You can substitute cheddar or Colby–Jack cheese for the pepper Jack, if you prefer, and top the popperettes with additional pickled jalapeños for a bigger burst of flavor.

Save Time: Bake these ahead and freeze in plastic freezer bags. To reheat, place 4 popperettes on microwavable plate. Cover with waxed paper. Heat on medium (50%) power 1 minute 30 seconds to 2 minutes 30 seconds or until hot.

SOUTHWESTERN SRIRACHA TUNA SLIDERS

PREP TIME: 25 minutes | **START TO FINISH:** 40 minutes | Makes 12 sliders

BISCUITS

- 2¼ cups Original Bisquick mix
- ½ teaspoon grated lime zest
- ¼ teaspoon ground cumin
- ⅔ cup milk

CUMIN-LIME BUTTER

- 2 tablespoons butter, melted
- ½ teaspoon grated lime zest
- ¼ teaspoon ground cumin

FILLING

- 1 can (5 oz) solid white tuna in water, drained
- ⅓ cup black beans, rinsed and drained (from 15-oz can)
- ⅓ cup cooked corn
- ¼ cup mayonnaise or salad dressing
- 1 tablespoon sriracha sauce
- 1 avocado, thinly sliced
- 3 slices (¾ oz each) cheddar cheese, cut into quarters

1 Heat oven to 450°F.

2 In medium bowl, stir Original Bisquick mix, lime zest and cumin until blended; stir in milk until soft dough forms. Place dough on surface sprinkled with Bisquick; roll in Bisquick to coat. Shape into a ball; knead 10 times. Roll dough ½ inch thick. Cut 12 biscuits with 2-inch round cutter dipped in Bisquick mix. Place on ungreased cookie sheet.

3 In small bowl, stir Cumin-Lime Butter ingredients until blended.

4 Bake 7 to 9 minutes or until light golden brown. Brush butter mixture over hot biscuits.

5 In medium microwavable bowl, stir together Filling ingredients except avocado and cheese. Microwave on High 1 to 1½ minutes, stirring halfway through, until hot. Split biscuits; set tops aside. Place bottom halves on ungreased cookie sheet. Spoon about 1 tablespoon Filling onto bottom of each biscuit; top with avocado slices and cheese.

6 Set oven control to broil. Broil with tops of sliders about 3 inches from heat 30 seconds to 1 minute or until cheese is melted. Top with biscuit tops. Serve immediately.

1 Slider Calories 210; Total Fat 11g (Saturated Fat 4g, Trans Fat 0g); Cholesterol 20mg; Sodium 360mg; Total Carbohydrate 20g (Dietary Fiber 2g); Protein 6g **Exchanges:** 1 Starch, ½ Other Carbohydrate, ½ Very Lean Meat, 2 Fat **Carbohydrate Choices:** 1

Kitchen Secret: Prefer chicken? Substitute canned chicken for the tuna.

Save Time: For quick assembly, make the Filling up to a day ahead. Cover and refrigerate until ready to use. Have the rest of the ingredients ready to go so the sliders can be assembled in minutes.

SAVORY CHICKEN FRIES

PREP TIME: 30 minutes | **START TO FINISH:** 45 minutes | Makes about 40 fries

CHICKEN FRIES

1	lb boneless, skinless chicken breasts
½	cup milk
1	egg
2	cups Italian-style panko crispy bread crumbs
⅔	cup Original Bisquick mix
1	teaspoon smoked paprika
1	teaspoon dried oregano leaves
½	teaspoon garlic powder
¼	cup butter, melted

DIPPING SAUCE

½	cup mayonnaise or salad dressing
¼	cup Dijon mustard
¼	cup honey

1 Arrange 2 oven racks in upper third and lower third of oven. Heat oven to 450°F. Line 2 large cookie sheets with foil; spray with cooking spray.

2 Cut chicken breasts lengthwise into ¼-inch strips. Cut strips lengthwise again to make long strips that look like French fries, about ¼ inch wide. Place in medium bowl.

3 In small bowl, beat milk and egg until blended. Stir 2 tablespoons of the egg mixture into chicken strips until coated. Reserve remaining egg mixture.

4 Place bread crumbs in shallow pan; set aside.

5 In 1-gallon resealable plastic food-storage bag, combine Original Bisquick mix, paprika, oregano and garlic powder; add chicken strips. Seal bag; shake to coat. Working with a few pieces at a time, dip coated chicken strips into remaining egg mixture, then coat with bread crumbs. Place in single layer on cookie sheets. Drizzle with butter.

6 Bake 10 to 12 minutes, turning chicken halfway through and alternating pans on oven racks, until chicken is no longer pink in center.

7 Meanwhile, in small bowl, stir together Dipping Sauce ingredients. Serve chicken with Dipping Sauce.

1 Fry Calories 80; Total Fat 4g (Saturated Fat 1.5g, Trans Fat 0g); Cholesterol 15mg; Sodium 180mg; Total Carbohydrate 7g (Dietary Fiber 0g); Protein 3g **Exchanges:** ½ Other Carbohydrate, ½ Lean Meat, ½ Fat **Carbohydrate Choices:** ½

Kitchen Secret: When coating foods with egg or other wet ingredients, and bread crumbs or other dry ingredients, it works best to make an assembly line of the dry coating, the wet mixture and the bread crumbs. Then use one hand to handle the dry ingredients and one hand to handle the wet ingredients.

Kitchen Secret: Serve a bunch of these as a quick dinner or as part of an appetizer spread. They are fun to pick up and dip and have a delightfully crisp exterior without having to deep fry!

QUICK LEMON-ROSEMARY NAAN

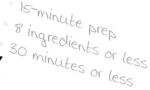

| PREP TIME: 15 minutes | START TO FINISH: 25 minutes | Makes 4 flatbreads |

1. In medium bowl, combine Original Bisquick mix, 1½ teaspoons of the lemon zest and 1½ teaspoons of the rosemary until blended. Stir in water, oil and yogurt; mix until soft dough forms.

2. On surface generously sprinkled with Bisquick mix, knead 10 to 12 times or until dough is soft and not sticky. Cover and let stand 10 minutes.

3. Heat 12-inch nonstick skillet over medium heat. Divide dough into 4 pieces. Using a rolling pin, roll each piece into 9×5-inch oval.

4. Brush 1 side of each naan with water. Place 1 naan in hot skillet, water side down. Brush top of naan with water. Cover and cook about 1 minute on each side or until golden brown. Repeat with remaining naan.

5. In small bowl, stir together butter, the remaining 1½ teaspoons of lemon zest and 1½ teaspoons rosemary. Brush over 1 side of each naan.

2	cups Original Bisquick mix
1	tablespoon grated lemon zest
1	tablespoon chopped fresh rosemary leaves
¼	cup warm water
1	tablespoon olive or vegetable oil
1	container (5.3 oz) plain Greek yogurt
2	tablespoons butter, melted

1 Flatbread Calories 340; Total Fat 14g (Saturated Fat 6g, Trans Fat 0g); Cholesterol 20mg; Sodium 630mg; Total Carbohydrate 44g (Dietary Fiber 1g); Protein 8g **Exchanges:** 1½ Starch, 1½ Other Carbohydrate, ½ Very Lean Meat, 2½ Fat **Carbohydrate Choices:** 3

Kitchen Secret: Naan is a leavened flatbread traditional in Asian and Indian cuisines. This shortcut naan can be used in place of a pita or as a sandwich wrap. It's also perfect to dip with hummus or tzatziki.

Kitchen Secret: Be sure you use plain Greek yogurt as directed. Greek yogurt has the excess whey strained out, which makes it thicker and creamier than regular yogurt. Plain Greek yogurt also has less sugar and more protein than regular yogurt. Don't use vanilla Greek yogurt, which is too sweet for these savory flatbreads.

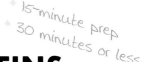

DILL PICKLE and HAM MINI MUFFINS

PREP TIME: 15 minutes | **START TO FINISH:** 30 minutes | Makes 24 muffins

1 Heat oven to 400°F. Spray 24 mini muffin cups with cooking spray.

2 In medium bowl, stir Original Bisquick mix, ham, dill pickles, dill weed and cream cheese. In small bowl, stir milk, pickle juice, oil and egg with fork or whisk until well blended. Make well in center of Bisquick mixture; stir in egg mixture just until dry ingredients are moistened. Divide batter among muffin cups, filling each until almost full.

3 Bake 10 to 12 minutes or until light golden brown and toothpick inserted in center comes out clean. Serve warm.

1 Muffin Calories 60; Total Fat 3g (Saturated Fat 1g, Trans Fat 0g); Cholesterol 15mg; Sodium 150mg; Total Carbohydrate 6g (Dietary Fiber 0g); Protein 1g **Exchanges:** ½ Starch, ½ Fat **Carbohydrate Choices:** ½

Kitchen Secret: If you like a little snap with your pickle, try spicy or hot dill pickles. It jazzes up the muffins with a bit of sweet heat.

Kitchen Secret: The dill plant provides both dill seed and dill weed used in cuisines worldwide. Dill weed, used in this recipe, are the leaves and are traditionally used as an herb. Dill seeds are the seeds of the dill plant and bring a more pungent, earthy flavor. If you are a fan of dill, sprinkle additional dill weed over the muffins before baking.

1½ cups Original Bisquick mix

½ cup chopped fully cooked ham

¼ cup chopped dill pickles

¾ teaspoon dried or ¼ teaspoon fresh dill weed

3 oz (from 8-oz package) cream cheese, cut into small cubes

⅓ cup milk

2 tablespoons dill pickle juice (from pickle jar)

1 tablespoon vegetable oil

1 egg

TWICE-BAKED GARLIC BREAD

PREP TIME: 15 minutes | **START TO FINISH:** 50 minutes | Makes 8 slices

¼ cup chopped
fresh parsley

1 tablespoon coarsely
chopped garlic

2 cups Original
Bisquick mix

2 tablespoons water

2 eggs

⅓ cup shredded
Parmesan cheese

3 tablespoons butter,
softened

1 Heat oven to 350°F. Spray cookie sheet with cooking spray.

2 In small bowl, combine parsley and garlic; reserve 2 tablespoons. In large bowl, stir remaining parsley mixture, Original Bisquick mix, water and eggs until soft dough forms.

3 Place dough on surface generously sprinkled with Bisquick mix; gently roll to coat. Shape into a ball; knead 10 to 12 times.

4 Shape dough into 8 × 3-inch loaf. Place loaf on cookie sheet. Flatten top of loaf slightly with fingers.

5 Bake 17 to 21 minutes or until light golden brown and toothpick inserted in center comes out clean. Let cool 15 minutes.

6 Cut bread in half horizontally. In small bowl, combine reserved parsley mixture, Parmesan cheese and butter. Spread cheese mixture on cut sides of bread.

7 Set oven control to broil. Broil with top about 6 inches from heat for 2 to 3 minutes or until topping is golden brown. Cut each loaf half crosswise into 4 slices. Serve warm.

1 Slice Calories 190; Total Fat 9g (Saturated Fat 4.5g, Trans Fat 0g); Cholesterol 60mg; Sodium 400mg; Total Carbohydrate 22g (Dietary Fiber 0g); Protein 5g **Exchanges:** 1 Starch, ½ Other Carbohydrate, ½ Medium-Fat Meat, 1 Fat **Carbohydrate Choices:** 1½

Kitchen Secret: If you prefer, use mozzarella or Italian blend cheese instead of the Parmesan cheese.

Kitchen Secret: Serve alongside your favorite soup, chili or pasta dish or with a main dish salad.

HAWAIIAN BUNS

PREP TIME: 15 minutes | **START TO FINISH:** 35 minutes | Makes 16 buns

3 cups Original Bisquick mix

½ cup packed brown sugar

¼ cup plus 1 tablespoon butter, melted

¼ cup pineapple juice

1 teaspoon vanilla

2 eggs

1 Heat oven to 400°F. Spray 9-inch square pan with cooking spray.

2 In large bowl, stir Original Bisquick mix, brown sugar, ¼ cup of the butter, the pineapple juice, vanilla and eggs until blended (dough will be soft).

3 Place dough on surface sprinkled with Bisquick mix. Scoop dough into 16 pieces (generous 2 tablespoons), rolling in Bisquick as necessary. Place rolls in pan. Brush with remaining 1 tablespoon butter.

4 Bake 14 to 18 minutes or until light golden brown. Serve warm.

1 Bun Calories 160; Total Fat 6g (Saturated Fat 3g, Trans Fat 0g); Cholesterol 35mg; Sodium 250mg; Total Carbohydrate 23g (Dietary Fiber 0g); Protein 2g **Exchanges:** 1 Starch, ½ Other Carbohydrate, 1 Fat **Carbohydrate Choices:** 1½

Kitchen Secret: A generous ⅛ cup measure or coffee scoop works well for shaping these rolls.

Kitchen Secret: For crunchy tops, sprinkle with coarse sugar or sanding sugar (or mix them, like we did here) before baking. These warm-from-the-oven rolls are great with butter and preserves or Cinnamon Smear (page 56).

Kitchen Secret: If you love Hawaiian dinner rolls, try this homemade quick bread version. They make a lovely side with chili or served as a breakfast bread with eggs and bacon.

DINNER IN A DASH

PIZZA WAFFLE GRILLED CHEESE

PREP TIME: 20 minutes | **START TO FINISH:** 20 minutes | Makes 4 sandwiches

½ cup ranch dressing

1 tablespoon pizza or Italian seasoning

4 Classic Waffles (page 18)

2 oz sliced pepperoni (from 6-oz package)

2 slices (¾ oz each) mozzarella cheese, halved

¼ cup sliced pitted ripe olives

¼ cup thinly sliced green pepper strips

1 tablespoon olive oil

1 In small bowl, mix ranch dressing and pizza seasoning; spread 1 tablespoon on one side of each waffle half; reserve remaining ranch dressing mixture.

2 Divide pepperoni, cheese, olives and peppers over dressing on 2 of the waffle halves. Top with remaining waffle halves, dressing side down.

3 In 10-inch skillet, heat 1½ teaspoons of the olive oil over low heat.

4 Place 1 waffle sandwich in hot skillet. Cook about 5 minutes on each side or until golden brown. Add remaining oil to the skillet; repeat with second sandwich. Cut waffles in half. Serve with reserved ranch dressing mixture.

1 Sandwich Calories 510; Total Fat 36g (Saturated Fat 9g, Trans Fat 0g); Cholesterol 65mg; Sodium 1,040mg; Total Carbohydrate 35g (Dietary Fiber 1g); Protein 11g **Exchanges:** 1 Starch, 1½ Other Carbohydrate, 1 High-Fat Meat, 5½ Fat **Carbohydrate Choices:** 2

Kitchen Secret: If you prefer, you can substitute pizza sauce for the ranch dressing and seasoning and serve with warmed pizza sauce for dipping. You can also try a different type of cheese; use whatever you have on hand.

Kitchen Secret: We've stuffed these sandwiches with several layers of fillings, so cooking them over low heat is important to get them perfectly melted and hot without the waffles getting too dark.

CHEESEBURGER CALZONES

PREP TIME: 20 minutes | START TO FINISH: 40 minutes | Makes 4 calzones

½ lb ground beef (at least 80% lean)
3 tablespoons ketchup
1 teaspoon yellow mustard
1 teaspoon dried minced onion
2 cups Original Bisquick mix
½ cup boiling water
1 cup shredded cheddar and American cheese blend (4 oz)
12 dill pickle slices
1 egg, beaten
1 teaspoon sesame seed

1 Heat oven to 375°F.

2 In 10-inch skillet, cook beef over medium-high heat 6 to 8 minutes, stirring occasionally, until thoroughly cooked; drain. Stir in ketchup, mustard and onion.

3 In small bowl, stir Original Bisquick mix and boiling water with fork until dough forms. Divide dough into 4 portions. Place dough on surface sprinkled with Bisquick mix; roll dough pieces in Bisquick mix to coat. Press each piece into 6-inch round, ¼ inch thick.

4 Spoon ¼ cup beef mixture onto one side of each dough round to within ½ inch of edge. Top beef with ¼ cup cheese and 3 pickle slices. Fold dough in half, covering filling. Press edges with tines of fork to seal. On ungreased cookie sheet, place calzones. Brush with egg; sprinkle with sesame seed.

5 Bake 15 to 20 minutes or until golden brown.

1 Calzone Calories 480; Total Fat 22g (Saturated Fat 10g, Trans Fat 0.5g); Cholesterol 110mg; Sodium 1,080mg; Total Carbohydrate 47g (Dietary Fiber 2g); Protein 23g **Exchanges:** 2 Starch, 1 Other Carbohydrate, 2 Medium-Fat Meat, ½ High-Fat Meat, 1½ Fat **Carbohydrate Choices:** 3

Kitchen Secret: After baking, top the baked calzones with more of your favorite burger toppings. Try lettuce, crumbled bacon, cheese and chopped tomatoes.

Kitchen Secret: These calzones are a perfect meal on the go. Simply wrap a baked calzone in foil to keep it warm while you're on the run.

BAKED TACO CHICKEN WINGS

PREP TIME: 15 minutes | **START TO FINISH:** 50 minutes | Makes about 5 servings (3 wings each)

1 Heat oven to 450°F. Fit large rectangular wire rack in 18 × 13-inch rimmed pan; spray both with cooking spray.

2 In large bowl, stir together Original Bisquick mix, oil, taco seasoning mix and salt until blended. Cut each chicken wing at joints to make 3 pieces; discard tip. Thoroughly pat chicken dry, add to mixture and turn to coat. Place in single layer on rack in pan.

3 Bake 30 to 35 minutes or until chicken is deep brown and juice of chicken is clear when thickest part is cut to bone (at least 165°F).

4 Meanwhile, in blender, place Herbed Sour Cream ingredients. Cover; blend on medium speed 30 to 60 seconds or until smooth. Serve with wings.

1 Serving Calories 500; Total Fat 37g (Saturated Fat 12g, Trans Fat 0.5g); Cholesterol 165mg; Sodium 970mg; Total Carbohydrate 16g (Dietary Fiber 1g); Protein 25g **Exchanges:** 1 Other Carbohydrate, 3½ Lean Meat, 5½ Fat **Carbohydrate Choices:** 1

Kitchen Secrets: For best results, pat chicken dry with paper towels before coating.

Kitchen Secrets: Using a wire rack allows air circulation around the wings, which creates a crispy texture. For best results, be sure to use a wire rack just smaller than your pan.

Save Time: The Herbed Sour Cream can be prepared up to a day in advance. Store covered in refrigerator.

WINGS
- ½ cup Original Bisquick mix
- ¼ cup vegetable oil
- 1 package (1 oz) taco seasoning mix
- ¼ teaspoon salt
- 3 lb chicken wings, thawed if frozen (about 15)

HERBED SOUR CREAM
- 1 carton (8 oz) sour cream
- 1 can (4.5 oz) chopped green chiles
- ¼ cup fresh cilantro leaves
- 2 tablespoons chopped green onions
- ¼ teaspoon salt

SPAGHETTI DUNKING STICKS

PREP TIME: 20 minutes | START TO FINISH: 45 minutes | Makes 4 servings (3 sticks each
+ ¼ cup sauce each)

8 oz bulk Italian
pork sausage

2 cups Original
Bisquick mix

1½ cups leftover cooked
spaghetti noodles, cut
into 3- to 4-inch lengths

½ cup water

¼ cup shredded
Parmesan cheese

1¼ teaspoons dried
basil leaves

2 eggs

2 tablespoons butter,
melted

⅛ teaspoon garlic powder

1 cup tomato pasta
or pizza sauce,
heated through

1 Heat oven to 400°F. Spray 9-inch square pan with cooking spray.

2 In 10-inch nonstick skillet, cook sausage over medium heat 4 to
5 minutes, stirring occasionally or until no longer pink; drain.

3 In medium bowl, stir cooked sausage, Original Bisquick mix,
spaghetti, water, 2 tablespoons of the Parmesan cheese,
1 teaspoon of the basil and the eggs until blended; vigorously beat
with spoon 20 strokes. Spread dough in pan.

4 In small bowl, stir together melted butter and garlic powder. Brush
garlic butter over dough; sprinkle with remaining 2 tablespoons
Parmesan cheese and ¼ teaspoon basil leaves.

5 Bake 15 to 18 minutes or until top is golden brown. Let stand
5 minutes.

6 With sharp knife, cut into 2 rows by 6 rows. Serve with
pasta sauce.

1 Serving Calories 530; Total Fat 23g (Saturated Fat 10g, Trans Fat 0g); Cholesterol 135mg;
Sodium 1,320mg; Total Carbohydrate 63g (Dietary Fiber 3g); Protein 19g **Exchanges:**
2 Starch, 2 Other Carbohydrate, ½ Vegetable, ½ Medium-Fat Meat, 1 High-Fat Meat, 2½ Fat
Carbohydrate Choices: 4

Kitchen Secret: This recipe is the perfect way to use up leftover
spaghetti. Add a tossed salad and your favorite fruit to round out
the meal.

Save Time: Plan ahead by freezing serving-sized portions of the
dunking sticks in an airtight container. To reheat, place 3 sticks on
microwavable plate; cover with waxed paper. Microwave on Medium
(50%) power 3 minutes 15 seconds to 3 minutes 45 seconds or until hot.

EASY BBQ CHICKEN BISCUIT SANDWICHES

PREP TIME: 20 minutes | START TO FINISH: 35 minutes | Makes 6 sandwiches

1½ cups Original Bisquick mix

1 cup shredded cheddar cheese (4 oz)

½ cup milk

2 tablespoons plus 1 teaspoon honey Dijon mustard

3 cups shredded deli rotisserie chicken

¾ cup barbecue sauce

2 tablespoons mayonnaise

2 cups shredded leaf lettuce

¾ cup sliced mini multicolored bell peppers

1 Heat oven to 425°F. Spray cookie sheet with cooking spray.

2 In large bowl, stir together Original Bisquick mix, cheese, milk and 2 tablespoons of the mustard until soft dough forms. Spread on cookie sheet into 7 × 5-inch rectangle. Cut dough in half lengthwise and in thirds on the long sides. Do not separate dough.

3 Bake 10 to 12 minutes or until golden brown. Cool 5 minutes before slicing.

4 Meanwhile, in medium microwavable bowl, stir together chicken and barbecue sauce. Microwave uncovered on High 3 to 4 minutes or until heated through.

5 In medium bowl, mix mayonnaise and remaining 1 teaspoon mustard. Add lettuce and bell peppers; gently toss to combine.

6 To assemble sandwiches, separate biscuit rectangle along cut lines. Cut each biscuit in half horizontally. Place bottom half on plate. Top each with ½ cup chicken and ⅓ cup lettuce slaw. Top with biscuit tops.

1 Sandwich Calories 440; Total Fat 20g (Saturated Fat 7g, Trans Fat 1g); Cholesterol 85mg; Sodium 1,360mg; Total Carbohydrate 37g (Dietary Fiber 1g); Protein 28g **Exchanges:** ½ Starch, 2 Other Carbohydrate, 3 Lean Meat, ½ High-Fat Meat, 1½ Fat **Carbohydrate Choices:** 2½

Kitchen Secret: Keep the dough from sticking to your knife by spraying the blade with cooking spray before cutting the dough.

Save Time: Make getting dinner on the table easier by making the biscuits ahead of time. Cool them on a wire rack and store tightly wrapped in the refrigerator up to 2 days. You can uncover and warm them in a paper towel in the microwave when you are ready to assemble the sandwiches.

EASY CHIPOTLE RANCH CHICKEN PIZZA

PREP TIME: 20 minutes | **START TO FINISH:** 30 minutes | Makes 8 slices

1 Heat oven to 400°F. Spray 12-inch pizza pan with cooking spray.

2 In medium bowl, stir Original Bisquick mix, ¾ cup of the cheese and the hot water with spoon until soft dough forms. Press dough evenly in pizza pan.

3 Bake 8 minutes. Spread dressing evenly over partially baked crust. Sprinkle 4 tablespoons of the cilantro and ¾ cup of the cheese on dressing. Top with chicken, tomato and remaining ½ cup of the cheese.

4 Bake 8 to 10 minutes or until edges of crust are golden brown. Sprinkle with remaining cilantro.

2	cups Original Bisquick mix
2	cups shredded pepper Jack cheese (8 oz)
½	cup hot water
⅓	cup chipotle ranch dressing
5	tablespoons chopped fresh cilantro
1½	cups shredded deli rotisserie chicken
1	cup chopped tomato

1 Slice Calories 330; Total Fat 20g (Saturated Fat 8g, Trans Fat 1g); Cholesterol 55mg; Sodium 770mg; Total Carbohydrate 22g (Dietary Fiber 1g); Protein 16g **Exchanges:** 1 Starch, ½ Other Carbohydrate, 1 Very Lean Meat, 1 High-Fat Meat, 2 Fat **Carbohydrate Choices:** 1½

Kitchen Secret: Spraying your fingertips lightly with cooking spray makes it easier to press dough in pan.

Kitchen Secret: If you don't have chipotle ranch dressing in your fridge, you can make your own by stirring ¼ teaspoon of chopped chipotle chile in adobo sauce or ground chipotle pepper into plain ranch dressing or skip the chipotle flavor and just use plain ranch dressing.

SPICY BEEF PIZZA PIE

PREP TIME: 10 minutes | **START TO FINISH:** 40 minutes | Makes 8 slices

1 Move oven rack to lowest position. Heat oven to 375°F. Spray 12-inch pizza pan with cooking spray.

2 In medium bowl, stir Original Bisquick mix, cheese sauce and hot water until soft dough forms. Place dough on surface sprinkled with Bisquick mix; roll dough in Bisquick mix to coat. Shape into a ball; knead 5 times or until smooth. Press dough into pan, using fingers dusted with Bisquick mix.

3 In large bowl, mix beef, salsa and beans; spoon mixture over dough to within 1 inch of edge. Top with tomato and green onions; sprinkle with cheese.

4 Bake 28 to 30 minutes or until crust is golden brown and cheese is melted.

2	cups Original Bisquick mix
¼	cup salsa-flavored processed cheese sauce
¼	cup hot water
½	pound cooked beef, shredded (about 1 cup)
1	jar (16 oz) thick and chunky salsa
1	can (15 oz) black beans, rinsed, drained
1	cup chopped tomato
4	medium green onions, sliced (¼ cup)
1	cup shredded pepper Jack cheese (4 oz)

1 Slice Calories 360; Total Fat 15g (Saturated Fat 7g, Trans Fat 0g); Cholesterol 40mg; Sodium 950mg; Total Carbohydrate 38g (Dietary Fiber 6g); Protein 16g **Exchanges:** 1 Starch, 1½ Other Carbohydrate, ½ Vegetable, 1 Very Lean Meat, ½ Lean Meat, ½ High-Fat Meat, 1½ Fat **Carbohydrate Choices:** 2½

Kitchen Secret: If you don't have cooked beef on hand, you can pick up shredded cooked beef in the refrigerated product section of the meat department at your grocery store or pick up beef barbacoa at the deli counter.

Save Time: If you have leftover beef from another meal, like a pot roast, you already have a jump start on this recipe. This recipe has a short prep time, just 10 minutes, because it starts with cooked beef.

THREE-CHEESE SPINACH FLATBREAD PIZZA

PREP TIME: 25 minutes | START TO FINISH: 35 minutes | Makes 5 servings (3 pieces each)

CRUST

- 1⅓ cups Original Bisquick mix
- ¼ cup grated Parmesan cheese
- ⅓ cup boiling water

TOPPING

- 2 tablespoons butter
- 1 bag (5 oz) fresh baby spinach leaves
- ¼ cup red onion pieces (1 × ¼ inch)
- 1 teaspoon finely chopped garlic
- ½ cup heavy whipping cream
- ½ cup grated Parmesan cheese
- ½ cup shredded mozzarella cheese (2 oz)
- 3 tablespoons crumbled feta cheese (about 1 oz)

1 Heat oven to 450°F. Spray cookie sheet with cooking spray.

2 In medium bowl, stir together Crust ingredients until soft dough forms. Gather dough into a ball. On cookie sheet, press dough into a 12 × 10-inch oval.

3 Bake 5 minutes.

4 Meanwhile, in 10-inch nonstick skillet over medium-high heat, melt butter. Add spinach, onion and garlic; cook 3 to 4 minutes stirring frequently until spinach is wilted. Remove spinach mixture from skillet; drain on paper towel–lined plate.

5 Wipe skillet with paper towel. In same skillet, add whipping cream. Cook over medium-high heat until mixture comes to a boil; boil 1 to 2 minutes stirring constantly until mixture thickens. Remove from heat; stir in ½ cup grated Parmesan cheese. Stir in spinach mixture.

6 Spread spinach mixture over flatbread. Sprinkle with mozzarella and feta cheese. Bake 5 to 6 minutes or until mozzarella cheese is melted. Cool 3 minutes. Cut into 5 rows by 3 rows.

1 Serving Calories 360; Total Fat 22g (Saturated Fat 13g, Trans Fat 0.5g); Cholesterol 60mg; Sodium 730mg; Total Carbohydrate 26g (Dietary Fiber 1g); Protein 13g **Exchanges:** 1 Starch, ½ Other Carbohydrate, 1 Vegetable, 1 Medium-Fat Meat, 3½ Fat **Carbohydrate Choices:** 2

Kitchen Secret: The skillet will be full when the spinach is added, but it cooks down quickly. Use nonstick tongs to toss the spinach until it is wilted.

Kitchen Secret: Add a little heat! Before serving, sprinkle the pizza with red pepper flakes.

MUFFIN CUP MEALS

Casseroles in a cup? This is a big idea in a small package. These tasty little meals make it easy to dine and dash on your busy nights.

Our recipes start on page 204. You'll love Sloppy Joe Muffin Cups and Philly Cheesesteak Muffin Cups for easy weeknight meals. Muffin-Cup Barbecue Bacon Meatloaves and Mini Corn Dog Muffins are fun and crazy-good. No matter which recipe you choose, you're headed for "Let's have this again!" status.

Make them ahead, if you like, and then reheat as many as you need. They're also perfect for little family members and a terrific choice for a hot lunch or a late-night snack. Maybe a double batch is in order?

Sloppy Joe Muffin Cups (page 204)

SLOPPY JOE MUFFIN CUPS

PREP TIME: 20 minutes   **START TO FINISH:** 40 minutes   Makes 6 servings (2 muffin cups each)

¾ lb ground beef (at least 80% lean)

1 cup original sloppy joe sauce (from 15-oz can)

¼ cup chopped red bell pepper

¼ cup chopped green onions

1 teaspoon chili powder

2 cups Original Bisquick mix

1 cup shredded Colby–Monterey Jack cheese blend (4 oz)

½ cup milk

1 Heat oven to 450°F. Spray 12 regular-size muffin cups with cooking spray.

2 In 10-inch nonstick skillet, cook ground beef over medium-high heat 5 to 7 minutes, stirring occasionally, until no longer pink; drain. Add sloppy joe sauce, bell pepper, onions and chili powder. Cook uncovered until mixture comes to boil, about 2 to 3 minutes, stirring occasionally; remove from heat.

3 In medium bowl, stir Original Bisquick mix, ½ cup of the cheese and the milk until soft dough forms. Form into a ball. Divide dough into 12 pieces. Press each piece in bottom and up sides of a muffin cup. Divide beef mixture among cups (about 1½ tablespoons each).

4 Bake 8 to 10 minutes or until crust edges are golden brown. Sprinkle with remaining cheese. Bake 1 to 2 minutes longer or until cheese is melted. Let stand 5 minutes. Run knife around edge of cups; carefully remove from pan.

1 Serving Calories 360; Total Fat 16g (Saturated Fat 7g, Trans Fat 0g); Cholesterol 55mg; Sodium 750mg; Total Carbohydrate 35g (Dietary Fiber 2g); Protein 18g **Exchanges:** 1 Starch, 1½ Other Carbohydrate, 1½ Medium-Fat Meat, ½ High-Fat Meat, 1 Fat **Carbohydrate Choices:** 2

Kitchen Secret: For a flavor and crunch explosion, top these baked muffin cups with your favorite flavor of coarsely crushed potato chips and pickle slices.

Save Time: Need a quick dinner? Make these ahead or freeze leftovers in freezer storage container. To reheat in the microwave, place 2 muffin cups on a microwavable plate; cover with waxed paper. Microwave on Medium (50%) 2 to 3 minutes or until hot.

PHILLY CHEESESTEAK MUFFIN CUPS

PREP TIME: 25 minutes   START TO FINISH: 50 minutes   Makes 6 servings (2 muffin cups each)

1. Heat oven to 400°F. Spray 12 regular-size muffin cups with cooking spray.

2. In 10-inch nonstick skillet, heat 2 tablespoons of the butter over medium-high heat. Cook and stir steak in butter 4 to 5 minutes or until no longer pink. Remove steak from skillet; drain and set aside.

3. In same skillet, melt remaining 1 tablespoon butter. Cook and stir mushrooms, bell pepper and onion over medium-high heat 5 minutes or until liquid from mushrooms evaporates and onion is tender. Stir in steak. Spoon slightly less than ¼ cup into each muffin cup.

4. In small bowl, stir Original Bisquick mix, milk, salt, pepper and eggs with fork or wire whisk until blended. Pour batter over ingredients in muffin cups; evenly divide cheese among muffin cups.

5. Bake 15 to 20 minutes or until knife inserted in center comes out clean. Let stand 5 minutes. Run knife around edge of cups; carefully remove from pan.

3	tablespoons butter
½	lb sirloin steak, cut into thin ¾-inch strips
1	cup sliced fresh mushrooms
¾	cup (1 × ¼-inch) bell pepper strips (1 medium)
1	medium onion, cut into thin strips
½	cup Original Bisquick mix
½	cup milk
½	teaspoon salt
¼	teaspoon pepper
2	eggs
1	cup shredded American cheese (4 oz)

1 Serving Calories 260; Total Fat 16g (Saturated Fat 9g, Trans Fat 0.5g); Cholesterol 120mg; Sodium 710mg; Total Carbohydrate 13g (Dietary Fiber 1g); Protein 16g **Exchanges:** ½ Other Carbohydrate, ½ Vegetable, 1½ Lean Meat, ½ High-Fat Meat, 1½ Fat **Carbohydrate Choices:** 1

Kitchen Secret: Serve with your favorite Philly cheesesteak toppings, such as ketchup, steak sauce, ranch dressing, sriracha sauce or sour cream.

Save Time: Freeze any remaining muffin cups in airtight container. To reheat, place 2 muffin cups on microwavable plate. Cover with waxed paper. Heat on Medium (50%) power 2 to 3 minutes or until hot.

MUFFIN-CUP BARBECUE BACON MEATLOAVES

PREP TIME: 20 minutes | **START TO FINISH:** 40 minutes | Makes 12 meatloaves

1 lb ground beef (at least 90% lean)
½ cup chopped cooked bacon
½ cup Original Bisquick mix
1 teaspoon barbecue seasoning
6 green onions, thinly sliced, whites and greens separated
1 egg
¼ cup barbecue sauce
3 slices (1 oz each) sharp cheddar cheese, quartered

1 Heat oven to 450°F. Spray 12 regular-size muffin cups with cooking spray.

2 In large bowl, stir beef, bacon, Original Bisquick mix, barbecue seasoning, green onion whites and egg until well mixed. Divide mixture among muffin cups, pressing evenly into cups.

3 Bake 14 to 17 minutes or until meat thermometer inserted in center of loaves reads 160°F. Brush loaves with barbecue sauce. Top with cheese. Bake 1 to 2 minutes longer or until cheese just melts.

4 Top with green onion greens.

1 Meatloaf Calories 140; Total Fat 8g (Saturated Fat 3.5g, Trans Fat 0g); Cholesterol 50mg; Sodium 260mg; Total Carbohydrate 7g (Dietary Fiber 0g); Protein 10g **Exchanges:** ½ Other Carbohydrate, 1½ Lean Meat, ½ Fat **Carbohydrate Choices:** ½

Save Time: You can slash time from your prep by purchasing precooked bacon crumbles rather than cooking your own bacon.

Kitchen Secret: If you like spicy foods, use spicy barbecue sauce or add a splash of red pepper sauce to the meat mixture.

MINI CORN DOG MUFFINS

15-minute prep
8 ingredients or less
30 minutes or less

PREP TIME: 15 minutes | **START TO FINISH:** 30 minutes | Makes 8 servings (3 muffins each)

1 Heat oven to 400°F. Spray 24 mini muffin cups with cooking spray.

2 In medium bowl, mix all ingredients except the hot dogs until well blended.

3 Evenly divide batter among muffin cups. Press 1 piece of hot dog horizontally into center of batter in each muffin cup.

4 Bake about 10 minutes or until light golden brown. Let stand 5 minutes; remove from muffin cups. Serve warm.

1 cup Original Bisquick mix
½ cup yellow cornmeal
¼ teaspoon salt
¼ cup milk
¼ cup butter, melted and cooled
3 tablespoons honey mustard
2 eggs
4 beef hot dogs, cut into ¾-inch slices

1 Serving Calories 270; Total Fat 18g (Saturated Fat 8g, Trans Fat 0.5g); Cholesterol 75mg; Sodium 500mg; Total Carbohydrate 21g (Dietary Fiber 0g); Protein 6g **Exchanges:** 1 Starch, ½ Other Carbohydrate, ½ High-Fat Meat, 2½ Fat **Carbohydrate Choices:** 1½

Kitchen Secret: Serve these corn dog cousins with additional honey mustard or ketchup. Or add a bit of pizzazz by using spicy brown mustard in place of the honey mustard and serving them with more spicy brown mustard, hot mustard or spicy ketchup.

Kitchen Secret: Here's a recipe that is fun for both kids and adults! It also makes a terrific party appetizer or after-school snack.

15-minute prep
8 ingredients or less
30 minutes or less

BAKED LEMON-PEPPER FISH

PREP TIME: 10 minutes | **START TO FINISH:** 30 minutes | Makes 4 servings

⅔ cup Original Bisquick mix

1 teaspoon Italian seasoning

1 teaspoon lemon-pepper seasoning

1 egg

2 tablespoons water

1 lb cod, haddock or other medium-firm fish fillets (about ½ inch thick)

2 tablespoons butter, melted

1 Heat oven to 425°F. Spray 15 × 10-inch pan with cooking spray.

2 In shallow dish, stir together Original Bisquick mix, Italian seasoning and lemon-pepper seasoning. In another shallow dish, beat egg and water. Dip fish into egg mixture, then coat both sides with Bisquick mixture. Place in pan. Drizzle with melted butter.

3 Bake 10 minutes. Turn fillets; bake 5 to 10 minutes longer or until fish flakes easily with fork.

1 Serving Calories 200; Total Fat 9g (Saturated Fat 5g, Trans Fat 0g); Cholesterol 110mg; Sodium 310mg; Total Carbohydrate 6g (Dietary Fiber 0g); Protein 22g **Exchanges:** ½ Starch, 3 Very Lean Meat, 1½ Fat **Carbohydrate Choices:** ½

Kitchen Secret: There will be a lot less coating on your hands if you use one hand to dip the fish into the egg mixture and the other hand to dip it into the Bisquick mixture.

Save Time: For an easy side, pair this fish with two-ingredient slaw. Stir together a bag of coleslaw mix and refrigerated coleslaw dressing for a quick accompaniment.

Kitchen Secret: Serve with lemon wedges and squeeze lemon over the fish just before serving. Top with cracked pepper.

EASY CHEESEBURGER-TOT CASSEROLE

PREP TIME: 20 minutes | START TO FINISH: 1 hour 5 minutes | Makes 8 servings (about 1½ cups each)

2 lb ground beef (at least 80% lean)

1½ cups chopped onion (1½ medium)

1½ teaspoons salt

½ teaspoon pepper

3 cups shredded cheddar cheese (12 oz)

1½ cups milk

¾ cup Original Bisquick mix

3 eggs, beaten

1 bag (32 oz) frozen potato nuggets

1 Heat oven to 400°F. Spray 13×9-inch (3-quart) glass baking dish with cooking spray.

2 In 12-inch skillet, cook beef and onion over medium-high heat 8 to 10 minutes, stirring frequently, until beef is thoroughly cooked; drain. Stir in salt and pepper. Spread in dish; sprinkle with 2 cups of the cheese.

3 In medium bowl, stir milk, Original Bisquick mix and eggs with whisk until blended. Pour into baking dish. Arrange frozen potato nuggets on top of casserole.

4 Bake 40 to 45 minutes or until potatoes are browned. Sprinkle evenly with remaining 1 cup cheese; bake 3 to 5 minutes or until cheese is melted and knife inserted in center comes out clean. Let stand 10 minutes before serving.

1 Serving Calories 690; Total Fat 42g (Saturated Fat 16g, Trans Fat 1g); Cholesterol 185mg; Sodium 1,500mg; Total Carbohydrate 42g (Dietary Fiber 3g); Protein 37g **Exchanges:** 1½ Starch, 1½ Other Carbohydrate, 3½ Medium-Fat Meat, 1 High-Fat Meat, 3 Fat **Carbohydrate Choices:** 3

Kitchen Secret: For the full cheeseburger experience, serve this dish with ketchup, mustard and pickles.

Save Time: If you cook up extra ground beef and onion while making a meal, you can have some on hand to make another meal in a snap. Simply cool the seasoned, cooked beef mixture; place in a resealable food-storage bag or freezer container and freeze up to 3 months. To use, simply thaw and continue as directed in the recipe or in other recipes calling for cooked ground beef and onion.

Save Time: Cook beef mixture; spread in baking dish. Refrigerate uncovered 30 minutes. Sprinkle with 2 cups of the cheese; pour Bisquick mixture over top. Cover and refrigerate overnight. To bake: Heat oven to 400°F. Uncover casserole; arrange frozen potato nuggets on top. Bake and top with cheese as directed.

SALSA CHICKEN BAKE

PREP TIME: 20 minutes | START TO FINISH: 45 minutes | Makes 8 servings

1 Heat oven to 375°F. Spray 13×9-inch (3-quart) glass baking dish with cooking spray.

2 In large bowl, stir Original Bisquick mix and milk until soft dough forms. Evenly drop half of dough by tablespoonfuls into bottom of baking dish (dough will not completely cover bottom of dish).

3 In 10-inch nonstick skillet, heat oil over medium heat. Stir in bell peppers; cook 2 to 3 minutes, stirring frequently, until just slightly crisp. Remove from heat. Stir in chicken, salsa and chili powder.

4 Spoon half of the chicken mixture over dough. Sprinkle with 1 cup of the cheese. Repeat layers with remaining dough, chicken mixture and cheese.

5 Bake 25 to 30 minutes or until golden brown and biscuits in center are cooked.

6 Top each serving with dollop of sour cream and cilantro.

3⅓	cups Original Bisquick mix
1	cup milk
1	tablespoon vegetable or olive oil
2	cups chopped green, red and/or yellow bell pepper (2 large)
2	cups cut-up cooked chicken
1	cup thick and chunky salsa
1	teaspoon chili powder
2	cups shredded Colby–Monterey Jack cheese blend (8 oz)
½	cup sour cream
2	tablespoons chopped fresh cilantro

1 Serving Calories 460; Total Fat 24g (Saturated Fat 10g, Trans Fat 1.5g); Cholesterol 65mg; Sodium 1,040mg; Total Carbohydrate 39g (Dietary Fiber 2g); Protein 22g **Exchanges:** 1½ Starch, 1 Other Carbohydrate, 1½ Lean Meat, 1 High-Fat Meat, 2 Fat **Carbohydrate Choices:** 2½

Kitchen Secret: To get cooked chicken the easy way, pick up rotisserie chicken. Remove meat from bones, cut it up and use immediately or place in a storage container. Store it in your freezer or refrigerator for later use. An average bird is about 2 pounds and yields 3 cups of cut-up meat.

Kitchen Secret: If you like colorful toppings, offer chopped tomatoes and avocado.

Save Time: While this yummy dish bubbles away in the oven, throw together a simple green salad or gather some crunchy veggies to round out and complement this homemade comfort food.

GLUTEN-FREE VEGGIE-STUFFED PEPPERS

PREP TIME: 40 minutes | START TO FINISH: 1 hour 30 minutes | Makes 4 peppers

1 Heat oven to 375°F.

2 Cut thin slice from stem end of each bell pepper. Remove seeds and membranes. If necessary, cut thin slice from bottom of each pepper so peppers stand up straight.

3 Place whole peppers in 8-inch microwavable baking dish. Add ¼ cup water; cover with plastic wrap. Microwave on High 3 minutes. Drain peppers; wipe out baking dish. Return peppers to baking dish. Spoon 1 tablespoon brown rice into bottom of each pepper.

4 Meanwhile, chop tops of pepper and any thin slices from bottom of pepper.

5 In 12-inch skillet, cook chopped bell pepper, mushrooms, onion and garlic in olive oil over medium heat 8 to 10 minutes, stirring occasionally, until vegetables are tender. Stir in spinach; cook and stir 2 to 3 minutes until spinach wilts and moisture evaporates.

6 In medium bowl, stir Bisquick Gluten Free mix, milk, salt, pepper and eggs until blended. Stir vegetable mixture and cheese into Bisquick mixture; divide among peppers.

7 Bake 40 to 50 minutes or until knife inserted in center of vegetable mixture comes out clean. Let stand 5 minutes before serving.

4 large bell peppers (about 8 oz each)
¼ cup uncooked instant brown rice
2 cups sliced fresh mushrooms
½ cup chopped onion
2 cloves garlic, finely chopped
2 tablespoons olive oil
1 bag (5 oz) fresh baby spinach leaves
½ cup Bisquick Gluten Free mix
½ cup milk
½ teaspoon salt
⅛ teaspoon pepper
2 eggs
1 cup shredded Asiago cheese (4 oz)

1 Pepper Calories 420; Total Fat 22g (Saturated Fat 9g, Trans Fat 0g); Cholesterol 125mg; Sodium 850mg; Total Carbohydrate 39g (Dietary Fiber 5g); Protein 17g **Exchanges:** 1 Starch, 4 Vegetable, ½ Medium-Fat Meat, ½ High-Fat Meat, 3 Fat **Carbohydrate Choices:** 2½

Kitchen Secret: When shopping for peppers, look for peppers with firm flesh without blemishes and that are about the same size. For stuffing peppers, it works best to find peppers that have flatter bottoms and can stand upright.

Kitchen Secret: The brown rice in this recipe absorbs excess moisture from the vegetables. It also adds texture and a bit of whole grain goodness, too.

Save Time: Peppers can be baked ahead and refrigerated. To reheat one pepper, place pepper on a microwavable plate; cover loosely with plastic wrap. Microwave on Medium (50%) 2 minutes 30 seconds to 3 minutes 30 seconds or until hot. Let stand 30 seconds.

EASY GREEK BEEF BAKE

PREP TIME: 25 minutes | **START TO FINISH:** 30 minutes | Makes 8 servings

1	lb ground beef (at least 80% lean)
1	teaspoon Greek seasoning
2½	cups Original Bisquick mix
1	cup milk
1½	cups shredded mozzarella cheese (6 oz)
1¼	cups chopped English (hothouse) cucumber
1¼	cups chopped tomatoes
¼	cup Italian dressing
½	cup crumbled feta cheese (2 oz)
2	tablespoons chopped fresh parsley

1 Heat oven to 400°F. Spray 13×9-inch (3-quart) glass baking dish with cooking spray.

2 In 10-inch skillet, cook beef over medium-high heat 5 to 7 minutes, stirring occasionally, until thoroughly cooked; drain. Stir in Greek seasoning.

3 Meanwhile, in medium bowl, stir together Original Bisquick mix and milk until soft dough forms. Pour and spread in baking dish. Spoon beef over dough.

4 Bake 14 to 16 minutes or until golden brown. Sprinkle with mozzarella cheese. Bake 2 to 3 minutes or until cheese is melted.

5 Meanwhile, in small bowl, stir together cucumber, tomatoes and dressing.

6 Spoon cucumber mixture evenly over mozzarella cheese. Sprinkle with feta cheese. Sprinkle with chopped fresh parsley.

1 Serving Calories 380; Total Fat 20g (Saturated Fat 8g, Trans Fat 1.5g); Cholesterol 55mg; Sodium 940mg; Total Carbohydrate 29g (Dietary Fiber 1g); Protein 21g **Exchanges:** 1 Starch, 1 Other Carbohydrate, 1½ Lean Meat, 1 Medium-Fat Meat, 2 Fat **Carbohydrate Choices:** 2

Save Time: Look for the Greek seasoning near the spices, dried herbs and seasonings in your supermarket. It's an easy way to get a lot of spices in a dish that you normally would have to buy and measure.

Kitchen Secret: What is an English cucumber? An English cucumber is the long, skinny cucumber that comes wrapped in plastic and is unwaxed. It is usually sweeter and less bitter than a regular cucumber and has a more tender skin.

Kitchen Secret: Top with a dollop of plain Greek yogurt, if you like.

EASY MUSHROOM-SWISS TURKEY BURGER PIE

PREP TIME: 15 minutes | **START TO FINISH:** 40 minutes | Makes 6 servings

½ lb ground turkey (at least 85% lean)

1½ cups mushrooms, sliced (about 5 oz)

¼ cup sliced green onions

1 teaspoon Montreal steak seasoning

1 cup shredded Swiss cheese (4 oz)

1 cup milk

½ cup Original Bisquick mix

2 eggs

1 Heat oven to 400°F. Spray 9-inch glass pie plate with cooking spray.

2 In 10-inch skillet, cook turkey, mushrooms and green onions over medium heat 8 to 10 minutes, stirring occasionally, until turkey is no longer pink. Stir in seasoning; spoon into pie plate. Sprinkle with ½ cup of the cheese.

3 In small bowl, stir milk, Original Bisquick mix and eggs with fork or whisk until blended. Pour into pie plate.

4 Bake 22 to 25 minutes or until knife inserted in center comes out clean. Sprinkle with remaining ½ cup cheese; let stand 5 minutes.

1 Serving Calories 220; Total Fat 12g (Saturated Fat 6g, Trans Fat 0g); Cholesterol 110mg; Sodium 320mg; Total Carbohydrate 11g (Dietary Fiber 0g); Protein 17g **Exchanges:** ½ Starch, ½ Vegetable, 1 Lean Meat, ½ Medium-Fat Meat, ½ High-Fat Meat, ½ Fat **Carbohydrate Choices:** 1

Save Time: This impossibly easy pie can be covered and refrigerated up to 24 hours before baking. You may need to bake a bit longer than the recipe directs since you'll be starting with a cold pie. Bake the minimum time and check for doneness, adding a few additional minutes until the doneness is reached.

Kitchen Secret: If you like, top with more green onion or try cooked bacon pieces or sliced or chopped tomato for a delicious topping.

EASY CHICKEN POT PIE

PREP TIME: 15 minutes | **START TO FINISH:** 45 minutes | Makes 6 servings

1⅔ cups frozen mixed
vegetables, thawed

1 cup cut-up
cooked chicken

1 can (10¾ oz) condensed
cream of chicken soup

1 cup Original
Bisquick mix

½ cup milk

1 egg

1 Heat oven to 400°F.

2 In ungreased 9-inch glass pie plate, stir vegetables, chicken and soup. In medium bowl, stir remaining ingredients until blended. Pour into pie plate.

3 Bake about 30 minutes or until crust is golden brown.

1 Serving Calories 230; Total Fat 9g (Saturated Fat 3g, Trans Fat 1g); Cholesterol 60mg; Sodium 670mg; Total Carbohydrate 25g (Dietary Fiber 3g); Protein 12g **Exchanges:** 1 Starch, ½ Other Carbohydrate, 1 Vegetable, 1 Lean Meat, 1 Fat **Carbohydrate Choices:** 1½

Kitchen Secret: You can change up this dish every time by varying the vegetables and type of condensed cream soup, depending on your taste and what's available in your pantry.

Kitchen Secret: If you have leftover cooked vegetables, use them instead of the frozen vegetables.

GLUTEN-FREE CHICKEN CLUB PIE

PREP TIME: 10 minutes | **START TO FINISH:** 45 minutes | Makes 6 servings

1 Heat oven to 400°F. Spray 9-inch glass pie plate with cooking spray without flour.

2 In pie plate, layer chicken, ham, bacon and cheese.

3 In medium bowl, stir milk, Bisquick Gluten Free mix, eggs and ¼ cup of the dressing with whisk or fork until blended. Pour over ingredients in pie plate.

4 Bake 25 to 30 minutes or until knife inserted in center comes out clean. Let stand 5 minutes.

5 Cut pie into wedges; top each wedge with lettuce and tomatoes. Drizzle with remaining ¼ cup dressing.

1 Serving Calories 280; Total Fat 13g (Saturated Fat 5g, Trans Fat 0g); Cholesterol 160mg; Sodium 730mg; Total Carbohydrate 17g (Dietary Fiber 1g); Protein 25g **Exchanges:** ½ Starch, ½ Other Carbohydrate, 3½ Very Lean Meat, 2 Fat **Carbohydrate Choices: 1**

Save Time: Save time by purchasing precooked bacon. Read the label to make sure it's gluten-free.

Save Time: Look for diced cooked chicken in the refrigerated or frozen section of the grocery store.

1½ cups diced cooked chicken
¼ cup diced cooked ham
4 slices gluten-free bacon, crisply cooked, crumbled
1 cup gluten-free shredded mozzarella cheese (4 oz)
1 cup milk
½ cup Bisquick Gluten Free mix
3 eggs, beaten
½ cup gluten-free light Caesar dressing
2 cups shredded romaine lettuce
1 cup cherry tomatoes, cut in half

BUFFALO CHICKEN POT PIE WITH CHEDDAR BISCUITS

PREP TIME: 35 minutes | **START TO FINISH:** 1 hour | Makes 8 servings

1 Heat oven to 350°F. Spray 8-inch square (2-quart) glass baking dish with cooking spray.

2 In medium bowl, mix chicken and sauce.

3 In 12-inch skillet, heat oil over medium heat. Add onion, celery and carrot; cook 6 to 7 minutes or until carrot is tender. Stir in chicken mixture and broth. Add cream cheese cubes and 1¼ cups of the cheddar cheese; stir until completely melted. Pour mixture into baking dish.

4 Meanwhile, in small bowl, mix Original Bisquick mix, milk, green onions and remaining ¼ cup cheddar cheese until well blended. Spoon 16 tablespoons dough on top of chicken mixture.

5 Bake 20 to 25 minutes or until casserole is bubbly and biscuits are golden brown.

1 Serving Calories 380; Total Fat 26g (Saturated Fat 12g, Trans Fat 0.5g); Cholesterol 90mg; Sodium 940mg; Total Carbohydrate 14g (Dietary Fiber 0g); Protein 22g **Exchanges:** 1 Starch, ½ Vegetable, 1 Very Lean Meat, 1 Lean Meat, ½ High-Fat Meat, 3½ Fat **Carbohydrate Choices:** 1

Save Time: Pre-chop your veggies when you have a few extra minutes, and store them in covered containers in the fridge up to a few days to skip the chopping time when making this dish.

Kitchen Secret: After baking, brush the tops of the biscuits with melted butter for extra flavor.

3 cups shredded deli rotisserie chicken (about 1 lb)

⅓ cup Buffalo wing sauce

1 tablespoon vegetable oil

1 cup chopped onion

1 cup chopped celery

½ cup chopped carrot

1 cup unsalted chicken broth (from 32-oz carton)

6 oz (from 8-oz package) cream cheese, cubed

1½ cups shredded cheddar cheese (6 oz)

1 cup Original Bisquick mix

⅓ cup milk

2 tablespoons sliced green onions

GLUTEN-FREE EASY TACO PIE

PREP TIME: 15 minutes | **START TO FINISH:** 50 minutes | Makes 6 servings

1   lb ground beef (at least 80% lean)

1   medium onion, chopped (½ cup)

1   package (1 oz) taco seasoning mix

1   can (4.5 oz) chopped green chiles, drained

1   cup milk

½   cup Bisquick Gluten Free mix

2   eggs

¾   cup gluten-free shredded Monterey Jack or cheddar cheese (3 oz)

¾   cup chopped tomato

1 Heat oven to 400°F. Spray 9-inch glass pie plate with cooking spray.

2 In 10-inch skillet, cook beef and onion over medium heat, stirring occasionally, until beef is brown; drain. Stir in seasoning mix. Spoon into pie plate. Top with chiles.

3 In small bowl, stir milk, Bisquick Gluten Free mix and eggs until blended. Pour into pie plate.

4 Bake about 25 minutes. Top with cheese and tomato; bake 2 to 3 minutes longer or until cheese is melted. Let stand 5 minutes before serving.

1 Serving Calories 290; Total Fat 16g (Saturated Fat 7g, Trans Fat 0.5g); Cholesterol 135mg; Sodium 520mg; Total Carbohydrate 17g (Dietary Fiber 1g); Protein 21g **Exchanges:** 1 Starch, ½ Vegetable, 2½ Medium-Fat Meat, ½ Fat **Carbohydrate Choices:** 1

Save Time: Cut up any ingredients you wish to top your pie with while it bakes. If you put them in small containers, your family can pick and choose their favorites!

Kitchen Secret: For the ultimate taco experience, serve with shredded lettuce, chopped tomatoes and sour cream. Don't be timid about using whatever favorite taco garnishes you have on hand, like sliced green onions, chopped black olives, guacamole, cooked corn or crushed corn chips.

CHICKEN ALFREDO SKILLET

PREP TIME: 20 minutes | START TO FINISH: 35 minutes | Makes 6 servings

1 tablespoon olive oil

1¼ lb boneless skinless chicken breasts, cut into 1-inch cubes

3 cups sliced zucchini (about 4 medium or 1 lb)

2 cups Original Bisquick mix

⅔ cup milk

½ cup shredded Parmesan cheese (2 oz)

3 tablespoons chopped fresh basil leaves

¾ cup Alfredo pasta sauce

1 cup chopped tomatoes

1 Heat oven to 400°F.

2 In 12-inch ovenproof skillet, heat oil over medium-high heat. Add chicken and zucchini. Cook 5 to 7 minutes, stirring occasionally, until chicken is no longer pink.

3 Meanwhile, in medium bowl, stir together Original Bisquick mix, milk, Parmesan cheese and 2 tablespoons of the basil until soft dough forms.

4 Stir Alfredo sauce into chicken mixture. Move mixture toward center of skillet. Drop 12 heaping tablespoonfuls of dough around edge of skillet.

5 Bake 12 to 14 minutes or until biscuits are golden brown. Spoon tomatoes over chicken mixture. Sprinkle with remaining fresh basil.

1 Serving Calories 470; Total Fat 24g (Saturated Fat 10g, Trans Fat 1.5g); Cholesterol 95mg; Sodium 840mg; Total Carbohydrate 33g (Dietary Fiber 2g); Protein 31g **Exchanges:** 1 Starch, 1 Other Carbohydrate, 1 Vegetable, 3½ Lean Meat, 2½ Fat **Carbohydrate Choices:** 2

Kitchen Secret: For extra color, use a combination of zucchini and yellow summer squash.

Kitchen Secret: You can change up the vegetables by using fresh broccoli florets and cut-up red bell pepper instead of the zucchini and tomatoes.

SLOW-COOKER CREAMY CHICKEN AND HERBED DUMPLINGS

PREP TIME: 20 minutes | START TO FINISH: 4 hours | Makes 8 servings

2½ lb boneless skinless chicken thighs (about 10 thighs)

3 cups chicken broth (from 32-oz carton)

4 medium carrots, peeled and cut diagonally into ¼-inch slices

3 stalks celery, cut diagonally into ¼-inch slices

1 medium onion, diced (½ cup)

1 teaspoon dried thyme leaves

½ teaspoon salt

½ teaspoon freshly ground black pepper

3 tablespoons cornstarch

2 tablespoons water

½ cup heavy whipping cream
Dumplings (page 42)

3 tablespoons chopped fresh parsley (1 tablespoon optional)

1 Spray 5-quart oval slow cooker with cooking spray.

2 In slow cooker, mix chicken, broth, carrots, celery, onion, thyme, salt and pepper. Cover; cook on High heat setting 3 to 4 hours or on Low heat setting 6 to 7 hours.

3 Uncover; using 2 forks, shred chicken into large chunks. If using Low heat setting, increase to High. In small bowl, beat cornstarch and water with whisk until smooth. Add cornstarch mixture and cream to slow cooker; stir to combine. Cover and continue to cook on High heat setting 20 to 25 minutes or until slightly thickened.

4 Meanwhile, prepare Dumplings, adding the optional 1 tablespoon parsley until soft dough forms.

5 Drop dumpling batter by 8 heaping tablespoons onto simmering chicken mixture in slow cooker. Cover and cook 20 to 25 minutes or until knife inserted into dumplings comes out clean.

6 Divide stew and dumplings into 8 serving bowls, and sprinkle with 2 tablespoons parsley. Serve immediately.

1 Serving Calories 400; Total Fat 17g (Saturated Fat 8g, Trans Fat 0g); Cholesterol 155mg; Sodium 970mg; Total Carbohydrate 27g (Dietary Fiber 1g); Protein 33g **Exchanges:** 1 Starch, ½ Other Carbohydrate, 1 Vegetable, 4 Very Lean Meat, 3 Fat **Carbohydrate Choices:** 2

Save Time: Cut up the veggies for this recipe the night before; cover and refrigerate them. Then in the morning, it's no effort at all to get this delicious dinner simmering away in your slow cooker!

Kitchen Secret: Don't worry if the chicken stew looks thin before you top with the dumplings. It thickens as the dumplings cook.

SWEET
TREATS
IN A SNAP

GLUTEN-FREE TOFFEE BARS

PREP TIME: 15 minutes | **START TO FINISH:** 1 hour 15 minutes | Makes 32 bars

1 cup butter, softened
1 cup packed brown sugar
1 teaspoon gluten-free vanilla
1 egg yolk
2 cups Bisquick Gluten Free mix
1 cup milk chocolate chips
½ cup chopped nuts

1 Heat oven to 350°F. Spray 13 × 9-inch pan with cooking spray without flour.

2 In large bowl, mix butter, brown sugar, vanilla and egg yolk. Stir in Bisquick Gluten Free mix. Press in pan.

3 Bake 20 to 25 minutes or until very light brown (crust will be soft). Remove from oven and immediately sprinkle with chocolate chips. Let stand about 5 minutes or until chocolate is soft.

4 Evenly spread chocolate over bars; sprinkle with nuts. Cool 30 minutes. Cut into 8 rows by 4 rows.

1 Bar Calories 150; Total Fat 9g (Saturated Fat 5g, Trans Fat 0g); Cholesterol 20mg; Sodium 125mg; Total Carbohydrate 15g (Dietary Fiber 0g); Protein 1g **Exchanges:** 1 Other Carbohydrate, 2 Fat **Carbohydrate Choices:** 1

Kitchen Secret: Three bars (1.55 oz each) gluten-free milk chocolate candy, broken into small pieces, can be substituted for the milk chocolate chips.

Kitchen Secret: After 30 minutes, the bars are still warm but not too hot to cut. We have you cut them then because it's easiest before they are cooled and set up.

EASY FROSTED BROWNIES

PREP TIME: 15 minutes | **START TO FINISH:** 1 hour 50 minutes | Makes 36 brownies

BROWNIES

- 6 oz unsweetened baking chocolate
- ¾ cup butter, softened
- 2 cups granulated sugar
- 1½ cups Original Bisquick mix
- 2 teaspoons vanilla
- 3 eggs

FROSTING

- 2 oz unsweetened baking chocolate
- ¼ cup butter, softened
- 2 cups powdered sugar
- 2 tablespoons milk
- 1 teaspoon vanilla

1 Heat oven to 350°F. Spray bottom only of 13 × 9-inch pan with cooking spray.

2 In small microwavable bowl, microwave 6 oz chocolate and ¾ cup butter uncovered on High 1 to 2 minutes, stirring every 30 seconds, until melted. Stir until smooth.

3 In medium bowl, stir together granulated sugar, Original Bisquick mix, 2 teaspoons vanilla, eggs and melted chocolate mixture until well blended. Spread in pan.

4 Bake 25 to 30 minutes or until edges begin to pull away from sides of pan. Cool completely, about 1 hour.

5 In medium microwavable bowl, microwave 2 oz chocolate uncovered on High 30 seconds to 1 minute, stirring after 30 seconds, until melted. Stir until smooth; cool 5 minutes. Stir in ¼ cup butter. Stir in remaining frosting ingredients until smooth and spreadable; if necessary, add more milk, 1 teaspoon at a time. Spread frosting over brownies. Let stand until set. Cut into 6 rows by 6 rows.

1 Brownie Calories 180; Total Fat 9g (Saturated Fat 6g, Trans Fat 0g); Cholesterol 30mg; Sodium 95mg; Total Carbohydrate 23g (Dietary Fiber 1g); Protein 2g **Exchanges:** 1 Starch, ½ Other Carbohydrate, 1½ Fat **Carbohydrate Choices:** 1½

Kitchen Secret: Unsweetened baking chocolate is bitter in flavor, making it the perfect choice for when you want a recipe chocolaty but not overly sweet. You'll find it in the supermarket in a rectangular box containing packages of 1-oz squares or bars.

Save Time: No softened butter on hand? Remove the wrapper and place in a small microwavable bowl. Microwave on 20% power for 30 seconds. Check softness and add more time in 10-second intervals, until softened but not melted.

EASY LEMON SUGAR COOKIE BARS

PREP TIME: 25 minutes | START TO FINISH: 1 hour 40 minutes | Makes 24 bars

BARS

3⅔	cups Original Bisquick mix
1	cup granulated sugar
1	cup butter, softened
2	teaspoons grated lemon zest
2	eggs

FROSTING

1	cup butter, softened
4	cups powdered sugar
2	teaspoons grated lemon zest
2	tablespoons fresh lemon juice
⅛	teaspoon salt

1 Heat oven to 350°F. Spray 13×9-inch pan with cooking spray.

2 In large bowl, mix Bar ingredients with spoon until soft dough forms. Press evenly into pan.

3 Bake 21 to 25 minutes or until golden brown. Cool completely, about 1 hour.

4 In medium bowl, beat 1 cup butter and 2 cups of the powdered sugar with electric mixer on low speed until blended. Beat in 2 teaspoons lemon zest, the lemon juice and salt. Gradually beat in remaining powdered sugar until well blended. If necessary, beat in additional lemon juice or water, 1 teaspoon at a time, until frosting is of desired spreading consistency.

5 Spread frosting over bars. Cut into 6 rows by 4 rows. Store tightly covered at room temperature.

1 Bar Calories 330; Total Fat 17g (Saturated Fat 10g, Trans Fat 0.5g); Cholesterol 55mg; Sodium 310mg; Total Carbohydrate 41g (Dietary Fiber 0g); Protein 2g **Exchanges:** ½ Starch, 2 Other Carbohydrate, 3½ Fat **Carbohydrate Choices:** 3

Kitchen Secret: Only 1 lemon is needed for this recipe. Zest it first, then cut in half and squeeze out the juice. If you have an orange, freshly squeezed orange juice and orange zest can be used in place of the lemon.

Kitchen Secret: To give your bars a fun look, try sprinkling with a variety of different-shape white and yellow decors immediately after frosting the bars.

GLUTEN-FREE ZUCCHINI, PEANUT BUTTER AND CHOCOLATE BARS

PREP TIME: 15 minutes | **START TO FINISH:** 1 hour 40 minutes | Makes 24 bars

1 Heat oven to 350°F. Spray 13×9-inch pan with cooking spray.

2 In large bowl, beat brown sugar, ⅓ cup peanut butter and butter with electric mixer on medium speed until well blended, scraping bowl occasionally. Beat in vanilla and eggs. Add Bisquick Gluten Free mix on low speed until mixed, scraping bowl occasionally. Stir in zucchini and chocolate chips. Spread in pan.

3 Bake 22 to 26 minutes or until golden brown around edges and toothpick inserted in center comes out clean. Cool completely, about 1 hour.

4 In medium bowl, combine Frosting ingredients until blended; frost bars. Cut into 6 rows by 4 rows. Store tightly covered at room temperature.

1 Bar Calories 270; Total Fat 11g (Saturated Fat 4g, Trans Fat 1g); Cholesterol 20mg; Sodium 220mg; Total Carbohydrate 38g (Dietary Fiber 1g); Protein 3g **Exchanges:** 1 Starch, 1½ Other Carbohydrate, 2 Fat **Carbohydrate Choices:** 2½

Kitchen Secret: Shred the zucchini with the coarse side of a grater and then pat with paper towels until most of the moisture is removed. Removing the excess moisture insures the bars won't be too wet.

Save Time: You can make these bars ahead. When completely cooled, frost as directed and cover tightly with plastic wrap or foil and freeze until you're ready for them. Uncover and thaw at room temperature and cut as directed.

BARS

- 1 cup packed brown sugar
- ⅓ cup gluten-free peanut butter
- ¼ cup butter, softened
- 1 teaspoon gluten-free vanilla
- 2 eggs
- 2 cups Bisquick Gluten Free mix
- 1 cup shredded zucchini, patted dry
- 1 cup miniature semisweet chocolate chips

FROSTING

- 1 container chocolate creamy, ready-to-spread frosting
- ⅓ cup gluten-free peanut butter

PECAN-COCONUT TOFFEE BARS

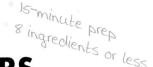

1 Heat oven to 350°F. Spray 8- or 9-inch square pan with cooking spray.

2 In large bowl, beat brown sugar and butter with electric mixer on medium speed about 3 minutes or until light and fluffy. Beat in Original Bisquick mix, scraping bowl occasionally, until blended. Evenly pat dough in pan.

3 Bake 25 to 35 minutes or until golden brown. Remove from oven and immediately sprinkle with chocolate chips. Let stand about 2 minutes or until chocolate is soft.

4 Spread chocolate evenly over bars. Sprinkle with coconut and pecans, pressing lightly to adhere to chocolate. Cool completely on cooling rack, about 1 hour 30 minutes. Cut into 4 rows by 4 rows.

¾ cup packed light brown sugar
½ cup butter, softened
2 cups Original Bisquick mix
¾ cup semisweet chocolate chips
⅓ cup flaked coconut
⅓ cup chopped pecans

1 Bar Calories 220; Total Fat 12g (Saturated Fat 6g, Trans Fat 1g); Cholesterol 15mg; Sodium 230mg; Total Carbohydrate 26g (Dietary Fiber 1g); Protein 1g **Exchanges:** ½ Starch, 1 Other Carbohydrate, 2½ Fat **Carbohydrate Choices:** 2

Kitchen Secret: These bars will have a crunchy texture once they cool completely.

Kitchen Secret: Change up the flavor of these bars simply by changing the nuts. Almonds, salted peanuts or macadamia nuts are all tasty options. Use what you have on hand.

15-minute prep

PUMPKIN BARS

PREP TIME: 15 minutes | **START TO FINISH:** 2 hours 45 minutes | Makes 48 bars

BARS

- 2 cups Original Bisquick mix
- 2 cups granulated sugar
- ½ cup vegetable oil
- 2 teaspoons ground cinnamon
- 1 teaspoon baking soda
- 4 eggs, beaten
- 1 can (15 oz) pumpkin (not pumpkin pie mix)
- ½ cup raisins

CREAM CHEESE FROSTING

- 3 oz (from 8-oz package) cream cheese, softened
- ⅓ cup butter, softened
- 1 tablespoon milk
- 1 teaspoon vanilla
- 2 cups powdered sugar

1 Heat oven to 350°F. Spray bottom and sides of 15 × 10 × 1-inch pan with cooking spray.

2 In large bowl, beat all Bar ingredients except raisins with electric mixer on low speed 30 seconds, scraping bowl frequently. Beat on medium speed 2 minutes, scraping bowl occasionally. Stir in raisins. Pour into pan.

3 Bake 25 to 30 minutes or until toothpick inserted in center comes out clean. Cool completely, about 2 hours.

4 In medium bowl, beat cream cheese, butter, milk and vanilla with electric mixer on low speed until smooth. Gradually beat in powdered sugar on low speed until smooth. Spread over bars. Cut into 8 rows by 6 rows. Store covered in refrigerator.

1 Bar Calories 130; Total Fat 5g (Saturated Fat 2g, Trans Fat 0g); Cholesterol 20mg; Sodium 95mg; Total Carbohydrate 19g (Dietary Fiber 0g); Protein 1g **Exchanges:** ½ Starch, 1 Other Carbohydrate, 1 Fat **Carbohydrate Choices:** 1

Kitchen Secret: For a more complex spice flavor, substitute 2 teaspoons of pumpkin pie spice for the ground cinnamon.

Save Time: Use a 16-oz container of cream cheese ready-to-spread frosting instead of making the scratch frosting.

MIX-IT-UP MUG TREATS

Craving a little sweet treat? These clever, two-serving snacks are made in mugs and microwaved in minutes. Throw on the toppings and, ohh, baby . . . you can be indulging in your very own mug treat faster than it takes to preheat your oven.

Our recipes start on page 248. Try our warm Cinnamon-Banana-Nut Mug Muffins for a fast, hot breakfast, or Caramel Candy Bar Brownie Mug Treats or Gluten-Free Upside-Down Citrus Cheesecake Mug Treats for a delicious snack or dessert. And there's also Strawberry-Rhubarb Oat Mug Treats, which could be for either breakfast or dessert—we'll let you decide!

- Use microwavable 12-oz cups.
- Microwave one mug at a time.
- Mixture will bubble up during cooking and then settle down.

CINNAMON-BANANA-NUT MUG MUFFINS

PREP TIME: 10 minutes | **START TO FINISH:** 15 minutes | Makes 2 muffins

⅓ cup Original Bisquick mix

¼ cup mashed ripe banana (about ½ banana)

3 tablespoons sugar

1 tablespoon butter, melted

1 tablespoon fat-free egg product

¼ teaspoon ground cinnamon

⅛ teaspoon vanilla

1 tablespoon chopped unsalted nuts (pecans, walnuts)

1 Spray bottoms of 2 microwavable mugs (about 12 oz each) with cooking spray.

2 In small bowl, stir Original Bisquick mix, banana, sugar, butter, egg product, cinnamon and vanilla until mixed well. Stir in nuts. Equally divide batter into mugs (about ⅓ cup batter each).

3 Microwave one mug at a time uncovered on High 45 to 60 seconds or until muffin top is set and edge pulls away from side of mug; let stand 1 minute before serving. Serve warm directly from mugs.

1 Mug Muffin Calories 260; Total Fat 10g (Saturated Fat 4g, Trans Fat 0g); Cholesterol 15mg; Sodium 250mg; Total Carbohydrate 40g (Dietary Fiber 1g); Protein 3g **Exchanges:** 1 Starch, 1½ Other Carbohydrate, 2 Fat **Carbohydrate Choices:** 2½

Kitchen Secret: Spraying only the bottom of the mug with cooking spray will make sure that your muffins get the proper height during microwaving.

Save Time: If you don't have egg substitute in your fridge, you don't have to run to the store. Instead, beat 1 egg, and measure out 1 tablespoon. Save the remaining egg to add to scrambled eggs or to make more mug muffins.

Kitchen Secret: Microwave ovens vary in cook times, so please start with the minimum cook time and add time as necessary.

CARAMEL CANDY BAR BROWNIE MUG TREATS

PREP TIME: 10 minutes | **START TO FINISH:** 15 minutes | Makes 2 mug treats

1. Generously spray 2 microwavable mugs (about 12 oz each) with cooking spray.

2. In small bowl, stir butter, sugar, vanilla and egg until well blended. Add Original Bisquick mix and cocoa; mix well.

3. Divide batter equally into mugs. Microwave mugs, one at a time, uncovered on High for 1 minute 15 seconds to 1 minute 30 seconds or until brownie top is set and brownie pulls away from side of mug.

4. Top each with 2 tablespoons chopped candy bar and 1 tablespoon caramel sauce.

¼ cup butter, melted
½ cup sugar
1 teaspoon vanilla
1 egg
½ cup Original Bisquick mix
2 tablespoons unsweetened baking cocoa
¼ cup chopped candy bar (any variety)
2 tablespoons caramel topping

1 Mug Treat Calories 730; Total Fat 33g (Saturated Fat 18g, Trans Fat 1g); Cholesterol 155mg; Sodium 620mg; Total Carbohydrate 99g (Dietary Fiber 3g); Protein 8g **Exchanges:** 1 Starch, 5½ Other Carbohydrate, ½ Medium-Fat Meat, 6 Fat **Carbohydrate Choices:** 6½

Kitchen Secret: It works best to microwave brownie mug treats one at a time. This ensures that the brownie will be cooked through.

Kitchen Secret: Make it extra delicious! Serve topped with whatever sprinkles you have on hand.

GLUTEN-FREE UPSIDE-DOWN CITRUS CHEESECAKE MUG TREATS

PREP TIME: 10 minutes | **START TO FINISH:** 1 hour 25 minutes | Makes 2 mug treats

4 oz (half of 8-oz package) cream cheese, softened

¼ cup sugar

3 tablespoons fat-free egg product

2 tablespoons heavy whipping cream

1 tablespoon Bisquick Gluten Free mix

¼ teaspoon grated lemon zest

¼ teaspoon grated orange zest

1 gluten-free vanilla sandwich cookie, chopped (from 10.5-oz package)

1 Spray bottoms of 2 microwavable mugs (about 12 oz each) with cooking spray.

2 In small bowl, mix cream cheese and sugar until smooth. Add egg product, whipping cream, Bisquick Gluten Free mix and lemon and orange zests; blend well.

3 Divide mixture evenly into mugs. Microwave, one at a time, uncovered on Medium (50%) for 1 minute 30 seconds, checking and adding an additional 10 to 20 seconds as necessary until top is nearly set (cheesecake center may look glossy); cool 10 minutes. Refrigerate until chilled, about 1 hour.

4 To serve, carefully run knife around edge of cheesecake to loosen; turn each onto small plate. Top with chopped cookie.

1 Mug Treat Calories 410; Total Fat 25g (Saturated Fat 15g, Trans Fat 1g); Cholesterol 75mg; Sodium 290mg; Total Carbohydrate 38g (Dietary Fiber 0g); Protein 6g **Exchanges:** ½ Starch, 2 Other Carbohydrate, ½ High-Fat Meat, 4 Fat **Carbohydrate Choices:** 2½

Kitchen Secret: For a beautiful presentation, serve these little cheesecakes with fresh berries.

Kitchen Secret: Leftover fat-free egg product? Use it to make Strawberry-Rhubarb Oat Mug Treats (page 251) or Cinnamon-Banana-Nut Mug Muffins (page 248), or use it to make scrambled eggs.

STRAWBERRY-RHUBARB OAT MUG TREATS

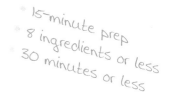

PREP TIME: 15 minutes | START TO FINISH: 20 minutes | Makes 2 mug muffins

1 Spray bottoms of 2 microwavable mugs (about 12 oz each) with cooking spray.

2 In small microwavable bowl, combine rhubarb, strawberries and 2 tablespoons of the brown sugar. Microwave uncovered on High 1 to 1½ minutes, stirring after 1 minute, or until fruit is softened. Reserve ¼ cup.

3 In another small bowl, stir together Original Bisquick mix, the remaining 2 tablespoons brown sugar, oats, butter and egg product until well mixed. Gently stir in remaining rhubarb mixture.

4 Equally divide batter between mugs. Microwave one at a time uncovered on High 1 minute 15 seconds to 1 minute 30 seconds or until muffin top is set and toothpick inserted in center comes out clean; let stand 1 minute.

5 Top each muffin with the reserved strawberry rhubarb mixture. Serve warm.

½ cup finely chopped fresh rhubarb

½ cup finely chopped strawberries

4 tablespoons firmly packed brown sugar

⅓ cup Original Bisquick mix

2 tablespoons quick-cooking oats

1 tablespoon butter, melted

1 tablespoon fat-free egg product

1 Mug Treat Calories 280; Total Fat 8g (Saturated Fat 4g, Trans Fat 0g); Cholesterol 15mg; Sodium 260mg; Total Carbohydrate 49g (Dietary Fiber 2g); Protein 3g **Exchanges:** 1 Starch, 1 Fruit, 1 Other Carbohydrate, 1½ Fat **Carbohydrate Choices:** 3

Kitchen Secret: Love streusel on your muffins? After topping each muffin with fruit mixture, sprinkle each with 1 tablespoon crunchy oat granola for a simple streusel hack!

Kitchen Secret: Make these a mug dessert! Top with a scoop of vanilla or cinnamon ice cream.

GLUTEN-FREE PEANUT BUTTER COOKIES

PREP TIME: 40 minutes | **START TO FINISH:** 2 hours 40 minutes | Makes 2½ dozen cookies

½ cup granulated sugar
½ cup packed brown sugar
½ cup gluten-free peanut butter
¼ cup shortening
¼ cup butter, softened
1 egg
1¼ cups Bisquick Gluten Free mix

1 In large bowl, mix sugars, peanut butter, shortening, butter and egg until blended. Stir in Bisquick Gluten Free mix. Cover; refrigerate about 2 hours or until firm.

2 Heat oven to 375°F.

3 Shape dough into 1¼-inch balls. Onto ungreased cookie sheets, place balls about 3 inches apart. With fork dipped in sugar, flatten balls in crisscross pattern.

4 Bake 8 to 10 minutes or until light golden brown. Cool 5 minutes; remove from cookie sheets to cooling racks.

1 Cookie Calories 110; Total Fat 6g (Saturated Fat 2g, Trans Fat 0g); Cholesterol 10mg; Sodium 90mg; Total Carbohydrate 13g (Dietary Fiber 0g); Protein 1g **Exchanges:** 1 Other Carbohydrate, 1 Fat **Carbohydrate Choices:** 1

Kitchen Secret: Want the perfect bumpy top on your cookies? Wipe off any excess dough and sugar that may collect between the tines of the fork when pressing the cookies.

Kitchen Secret: For a special treat, sandwich two of these all-time favorites together with a scoop of chocolate ice cream. Roll the edge in chopped gluten-free candy bar or nuts.

GLUTEN-FREE CHOCOLATE CRINKLES

PREP TIME: 1 hour 20 minutes | **START TO FINISH:** 4 hours 20 minutes | Makes 6 dozen cookies

2 cups granulated sugar
½ cup vegetable oil
2 teaspoons gluten-free vanilla
4 oz unsweetened baking chocolate, melted, cooled
4 eggs
2½ cups Bisquick Gluten Free mix
½ cup powdered sugar

1 In large bowl, mix sugar, oil, vanilla and chocolate. Stir in eggs, one at a time. Stir in Bisquick Gluten Free mix until dough forms. Cover; refrigerate at least 3 hours.

2 Heat oven to 350°F. Spray cookie sheets with cooking spray without flour.

3 Drop dough by teaspoonfuls into powdered sugar; roll around to coat and shape into balls. Onto cookie sheets, place balls about 2 inches apart.

4 Bake 10 to 12 minutes or until almost no imprint remains when touched lightly in center. Immediately remove from cookie sheets to cooling racks.

1 Cookie Calories 60; Total Fat 2g (Saturated Fat 0g, Trans Fat 0g); Cholesterol 10mg; Sodium 50mg; Total Carbohydrate 10g (Dietary Fiber 0g); Protein 0g **Exchanges:** ½ Other Carbohydrate, ½ Fat **Carbohydrate Choices:** ½

Save Time: Line cookie sheets with foil. Simply bake cookies as directed, spraying the foil as you would the cookie sheet. Then throw the foil away—no need to wash the pan!

Save Time: Save time and dishes by melting the chocolate in the bowl used to mix with the other ingredients. In a large microwavable bowl, microwave chocolate uncovered on High 30 seconds to 1 minute, stirring after 30 seconds, until melted. Stir until smooth. Continue as directed in step 1.

GLUTEN-FREE SNICKERDOODLES

PREP TIME: 15 minutes | **START TO FINISH:** 50 minutes | Makes 2½ dozen cookies

1 Heat oven to 375°F.

2 In large bowl, mix 1 cup of the sugar, the butter, shortening and eggs. Stir in Bisquick Gluten Free mix until dough forms.

3 In small bowl, mix remaining ¼ cup sugar and the cinnamon. Shape dough into 1¼-inch balls; roll balls in sugar-cinnamon mixture. Onto ungreased cookie sheets, place balls 2 inches apart.

4 Bake 10 to 12 minutes or until set. Immediately remove from cookie sheets to cooling racks.

1¼	cups sugar
¼	cup butter, softened
¼	cup shortening
2	eggs
2	cups Bisquick Gluten Free mix
2	teaspoons ground cinnamon

1 Cookie Calories 100; Total Fat 3.5g (Saturated Fat 1.5g, Trans Fat 0g); Cholesterol 20mg; Sodium 105mg; Total Carbohydrate 15g (Dietary Fiber 0g); Protein 1g **Exchanges:** ½ Starch, ½ Other Carbohydrate, ½ Fat **Carbohydrate Choices:** 1

Kitchen Secret: If the dough feels too soft for shaping into balls, put dough in freezer for 10 to 15 minutes to firm it up.

Save Time: Streamline cookie making by scooping the dough with a spring-handled ice-cream scoop. A #50 scoop is what you'll want to use to get 1¼-inch balls. Ice-cream scoops are a great multiuse kitchen tool that comes in a variety of sizes.

GLUTEN-FREE RUSSIAN TEA CAKES

PREP TIME: 1 hour | **START TO FINISH:** 1 hour 25 minutes | Makes 4 dozen cookies

1 Heat oven to 400°F.

2 In large bowl, mix butter, ½ cup of the powdered sugar, the vanilla and egg. Stir in Bisquick Gluten Free mix and nuts until dough holds together.

3 Shape dough into 1-inch balls. Onto ungreased cookie sheets, place balls about 1 inch apart.

4 Bake 9 to 11 minutes or until set but not brown. Immediately remove from cookie sheets to cooling racks. Cool slightly.

5 Roll warm cookies in the remaining ⅔ cup powdered sugar; place on cooling racks to cool completely. Roll in powdered sugar again.

1	cup butter, softened
½	cup plus ⅔ cup powdered sugar
1	teaspoon gluten-free vanilla
1	egg
2¼	cups Bisquick Gluten Free mix
¾	cup finely chopped nuts

1 Cookie Calories 80; Total Fat 5g (Saturated Fat 2.5g, Trans Fat 0g); Cholesterol 15mg; Sodium 95mg; Total Carbohydrate 9g (Dietary Fiber 0g); Protein 0g **Exchanges:** ½ Other Carbohydrate, 1 Fat **Carbohydrate Choices:** ½

Kitchen Secret: Our favorite nuts for these rich little balls are pecans or walnuts. Macadamia nuts are another great choice.

Kitchen Secret: Rolling the balls in powdered sugar twice helps to get enough on the cookies: once while the cookies are hot, to get it to stick to the cookies, and then the second time when the cookies are cooled, to stick to the first layer.

DOUBLE-ALMOND CHURRO BALLS

PREP TIME: 45 minutes | **START TO FINISH:** 45 minutes | Makes about 70 churro balls

Vegetable oil for deep-frying
¼ cup plus 1 tablespoon sugar
3½ cups Original Bisquick mix
½ cup ground almonds
1 cup hot water
1 tablespoon almond extract

1 In 2-quart saucepan, place 2 inches of vegetable oil. Heat over medium-high heat until deep-fry thermometer reads 375°F.

2 Meanwhile, place ¼ cup of the sugar in lunch paper bag or food-storage plastic bag; set aside. In medium bowl, stir together Original Bisquick mix, almonds and the remaining 1 tablespoon sugar. In small bowl, mix hot water and almond extract; stir into dry ingredients until soft dough forms.

3 To make churros, use resealable freezer plastic bag with 1-inch hole cut in 1 bottom corner or a decorating bag with 1-inch hole. Working in batches, spoon dough into bag; seal bag (twist or fold top of decorating bag).

4 Holding bag with one hand and carefully cutting dough with scissors, drop dough by 1½-inch pieces into hot oil. Fry several pieces at one time, but do not crowd them (the pieces will become balls). Fry 1 minute 30 seconds to 2 minutes, turning once, until center is fully cooked and balls are golden brown.

5 Place churro balls in paper bag with sugar; shake to coat. Serve warm.

1 Churro Ball Calories 60; Total Fat 3.5g (Saturated Fat 0.5g, Trans Fat 0g); Cholesterol 0mg; Sodium 75mg; Total Carbohydrate 5g (Dietary Fiber 0g); Protein 0g **Exchanges:** ½ Starch, ½ Fat **Carbohydrate Choices:** ½

Save Time: Using a bag allows you to coat several balls at one time.
Kitchen Secret: Be sure to allow your oil to come back to 375°F between batches so that the churros don't become heavy with oil when fried.

15-minute prep

CRANBERRY UPSIDE-DOWN CAKE

PREP TIME: 15 minutes | START TO FINISH: 1 hour 15 minutes | Makes 8 servings

TOPPING

- ⅓ cup packed brown sugar
- ¼ cup butter, melted
- 1¼ cups fresh or frozen (thawed) cranberries

CAKE

- 1½ cups Original Bisquick mix
- ½ cup granulated sugar
- ½ cup milk
- 2 tablespoons vegetable oil
- 1 teaspoon vanilla
- 1 egg

1 Heat oven to 350°F. Spray 8-inch round cake pan with cooking spray; line with cooking parchment paper.

2 In cake pan, stir brown sugar and butter until well blended. Sprinkle cranberries over brown sugar mixture; set aside.

3 In large bowl, beat Cake ingredients with electric mixer on low speed 30 seconds, scraping bowl constantly. Beat on medium speed 4 minutes, scraping bowl occasionally. Pour batter over cranberries in pan.

4 Bake 33 to 38 minutes or until deep golden brown and toothpick inserted in center comes out clean.

5 Run knife around side of pan to loosen cake. Cool on cooling rack 5 minutes. Place heatproof serving plate upside down over pan; turn plate and pan over. Remove pan. Cool 15 minutes before serving.

6 Cut into wedges. Store loosely covered in refrigerator.

1 Serving Calories 280; Total Fat 12g (Saturated Fat 5g, Trans Fat 0g); Cholesterol 40mg; Sodium 280mg; Total Carbohydrate 40g (Dietary Fiber 1g); Protein 3g **Exchanges:** 1 Starch, 1½ Other Carbohydrate, 2½ Fat **Carbohydrate Choices:** 2½

Kitchen Secret: To ensure baking success, be sure to beat Cake ingredients for the full 4 minutes.

Kitchen Secret: Serve wedges with whipped cream! Make your own— it's easy! In a chilled medium bowl, beat ¾ cup heavy whipping cream and 1 tablespoon powdered sugar with electric mixer on high speed until mixture begins to thicken. Add ½ teaspoon vanilla; beat on high speed until whipped cream forms soft peaks. You can shortcut this by using purchased whipped cream topping, if you like.

Kitchen Secret: When fresh cranberries are available, stock up with an extra bag or two. They can be stored in your freezer for up to a year!

PUMPKIN STREUSEL COFFEE CAKE

PREP TIME: 15 minutes | **START TO FINISH:** 1 hour 10 minutes | Makes 16 servings

STREUSEL

- 1 cup Original Bisquick mix
- 1 cup old-fashioned oats
- ½ cup packed brown sugar
- ½ cup cold butter, cut in pieces

CAKE

- 1½ cups Original Bisquick mix
- 2 teaspoons pumpkin pie spice
- 2 eggs, slightly beaten
- ½ cup granulated sugar
- ½ cup canned pumpkin (not pumpkin pie mix)
- ¼ cup milk
- 2 tablespoons vegetable oil

1 Heat oven to 350°F. Spray 9-inch square pan with cooking spray.

2 In medium bowl, mix 1 cup Original Bisquick mix, oats and brown sugar. Cut in butter, using fork or pastry blender, until mixture is crumbly; set aside.

3 In small bowl, mix 1½ cups Bisquick mix and pumpkin pie spice; set aside. In medium bowl, beat eggs, granulated sugar, pumpkin, milk and oil with whisk until well blended. Beat in Bisquick and spice mixture until blended. Pour batter in pan. Sprinkle Streusel over top.

4 Bake 30 to 35 minutes or until toothpick inserted in center comes out clean. Let stand 20 minutes.

5 Cut into 4 rows by 4 rows. Store loosely covered.

1 Serving Calories 220; Total Fat 10g (Saturated Fat 4.5g, Trans Fat 0g); Cholesterol 40mg; Sodium 240mg; Total Carbohydrate 31g (Dietary Fiber 1g); Protein 3g **Exchanges:** 1 Starch, 1 Other Carbohydrate, 2 Fat **Carbohydrate Choices:** 2

Kitchen Secret: You can freeze leftover pumpkin in an airtight container for your favorite recipes. Just thaw and stir before adding.

Kitchen Secret: Pumpkin pie spice is a staple spice in many fall recipes, and it's easy to make your own: Mix 3 tablespoons ground cinnamon, 2 teaspoons ground ginger, 2 teaspoons ground nutmeg, 1½ teaspoons ground allspice and 1½ teaspoons ground cloves. Mix the spices, and store mixture in a clean small jar.

MINI WHOOPIE PIES

PREP TIME: 1 hour | **START TO FINISH:** 1 hour | Makes 25 whoopie pies

1 Heat oven to 350°F. Line two large cookie sheets with cooking parchment paper.

2 In medium bowl, beat granulated sugar and 2 tablespoons butter with electric mixer on low speed until well blended and sandy in texture. Add remaining cookie ingredients except food color. Beat on medium speed 2 minutes, scraping bowl occasionally, until smooth.

3 Stir food color into batter as desired to create bright-red color. Stir until well blended. Spoon batter into resealable food-storage plastic bag. Cut ½ inch off corner of bag. Onto cookie sheets, gently squeeze bag of batter to make about fifty 1-inch circles of dough (about ½ teaspoon each), about 1 inch apart.

4 Bake 7 to 8 minutes or until tops spring back when lightly touched. Cool 2 minutes; gently remove from cookie sheets and place on cooling racks. Cool completely, about 20 minutes.

5 Meanwhile, in medium bowl, beat Filling ingredients except powdered sugar with electric mixer on low speed until well mixed. Gradually add powdered sugar, beating on low speed until incorporated. Increase speed to medium; beat about 1 minute or until smooth.

6 For each whoopie pie, spread about 1 teaspoon filling on bottom of 1 cookie; place second cookie, bottom side down, on filling. Store loosely covered in refrigerator.

COOKIES

½	cup granulated sugar
2	tablespoons butter, softened
1½	cups Original Bisquick mix
⅓	cup milk
1	teaspoon vanilla
1	egg
	Red gel food color

FILLING

4	oz (half of 8-oz package) cream cheese, softened
¼	cup butter, softened
½	teaspoon vanilla
1¼	cups powdered sugar

1 Whoopie Pie Calories 60; Total Fat 2.5g (Saturated Fat 1.5g, Trans Fat 0g); Cholesterol 10mg; Sodium 70mg; Total Carbohydrate 8g (Dietary Fiber 0g); Protein 0g **Exchanges:** ½ Other Carbohydrate, ½ Fat **Carbohydrate Choices:** ½

Kitchen Secret: Try to keep the whoopie pies the same size so they will bake evenly.

Kitchen Secret: What can you do with the leftover cream cheese? Spread it on bagels or top it with some preserves or salsa to serve with crackers or tortilla chips.

Save Time: If you prefer, omit the filling and use cream cheese ready-to-spread frosting between the cookies. If you use the frosting, there is no need to refrigerate during storage.

WAFFLE CONE ICE-CREAM SUNDAES

PREP TIME: 30 minutes | **START TO FINISH:** 1 hour | Makes 6 sundae cones

1. Heat oven to 350°F. Make forms for waffle cones by crumpling each foil piece into a 5-inch cone, about 3 inches in diameter.

2. Brush waffle maker with vegetable oil or spray with cooking spray. Heat waffle maker.

3. In medium bowl, mix Waffle Cone ingredients.

4. For each cone, pour ⅓ cup batter onto center of hot waffle maker. Close lid of waffle maker. Bake about 1½ minutes or until waffle is golden brown. Carefully remove waffle to cooling rack; immediately gently press waffle with rolling pin to flatten.

5. Form waffle over outside of foil cone, extending waffle beyond tip of foil, pressing lightly to shape, overlapping slightly. Gently press waffle together at point of cone. Place cone, seam side down, on ungreased cookie sheet or baking pan. Repeat with remaining waffle batter and foil cones.

6. Bake 18 to 22 minutes or until waffle is dry. Remove cones with foil to cooling rack. Let stand 5 minutes. Carefully remove foil. Cool completely, about 15 minutes.

7. Place candy pieces in bottom of waffle. Scoop ice cream into cones; top with ice-cream topping.

6 (15×12-inch) pieces aluminum foil

WAFFLE CONES

2 cups Original Bisquick mix

1 cup milk

2 tablespoons sugar

2 tablespoons vegetable oil

1 teaspoon vanilla

1 egg

ICE CREAM AND TOPPINGS

2 tablespoons candy-coated chocolate pieces

6 scoops ice cream (about ½ cup each)

6 tablespoons chocolate or caramel ice-cream topping

1 Sundae Cone Calories 460; Total Fat 18g (Saturated Fat 8g, Trans Fat 0g); Cholesterol 65mg; Sodium 480mg; Total Carbohydrate 66g (Dietary Fiber 2g); Protein 8g **Exchanges:** 1 Starch, 3 Other Carbohydrate, ½ Milk, 2½ Fat **Carbohydrate Choices:** 4½

Save Time: Cones can be made ahead and frozen in resealable gallon-size freezer bags. To thaw, remove from bag and let stand at room temperature 30 minutes.

Kitchen Secret: Create over-the-top, picture-worthy cones. For a fancier presentation, dip edges in melted candy coating and sprinkle with colorful sprinkles or decors. Let dry before filling. When filling cones, sprinkle ice cream with additional candies or sprinkles and thread marshmallows and cut-up candy bars onto a 6- or 8-inch wooden skewer and poke into ice cream. Or top with whipped cream and a maraschino cherry.

Kitchen Secret: Placing a small piece of candy, such as a malted milk ball or a few candy-coated chocolate pieces, as we have done, helps keep ice cream from melting through the tip of the cone.

STRAWBERRY-BASIL SLAB SHORTCAKE

PREP TIME: 30 minutes | START TO FINISH: 1 hour 10 minutes | Makes 12 servings

SHORTCAKE

- 3½ cups Original Bisquick mix
- ¾ cup milk
- ¼ cup granulated sugar
- 2 tablespoons chopped fresh basil leaves
- 4 oz (half of 8-oz package) cream cheese, softened

STRAWBERRY-BASIL TOPPING

- 1 quart (4 cups) strawberries, sliced
- ¼ cup granulated sugar
- 1 tablespoon julienne strips fresh basil leaves

WHIPPED CREAM CHEESE

- 1 package (8 oz) cream cheese, softened
- 1 cup heavy whipping cream
- ⅓ cup powdered sugar
- 1 teaspoon vanilla

1 Heat oven to 400°F.

2 In large bowl, stir all Shortcake ingredients until soft dough forms. Using fingers dusted with Bisquick, press dough in bottom of 15 × 10 × 1-inch ungreased pan.

3 Bake 14 to 16 minutes or until golden brown. Cool completely, about 45 minutes.

4 Meanwhile, in large bowl, mix Strawberry-Basil Topping ingredients; stir occasionally until ready to assemble shortcake.

5 In medium bowl, beat Whipped Cream Cheese ingredients with electric mixer on medium-high speed until mixture is thickened. Spread over top of shortcake. Using slotted spoon, spoon Strawberry-Basil Topping over cream cheese. Cut into 4 rows by 3 rows. Store any remaining shortcake covered in refrigerator.

1 Serving Calories 370; Total Fat 19g (Saturated Fat 11g, Trans Fat 0.5g); Cholesterol 50mg; Sodium 440mg; Total Carbohydrate 44g (Dietary Fiber 2g); Protein 5g **Exchanges:** ½ Starch, 2½ Other Carbohydrate, ½ High-Fat Meat, 3 Fat **Carbohydrate Choices:** 3

Kitchen Secret: If you like, drizzle a little balsamic glaze over the strawberries before serving or set out a small container of it and let guests drizzle it themselves or garnish with some sprigs of fresh basil.

Save Time: You can easily prepare this summer dessert ahead. Both the shortcake and the strawberries can be made early in the day. If you are making it in the morning, store strawberries in the refrigerator. When ready to serve, continue with step 5. If you prefer, you can also frost the shortcake and store in the refrigerator. When ready to serve, spoon strawberries over the cream cheese topping.

IMPOSSIBLY EASY PUMPKIN PIE

PREP TIME: 10 minutes | START TO FINISH: 3 hours 20 minutes | Makes 6 servings

1	cup canned pumpkin (not pumpkin pie mix)
1	cup evaporated milk
½	cup Original Bisquick mix
½	cup sugar
1	tablespoon butter, softened
1½	teaspoons pumpkin pie spice
1	teaspoon vanilla
2	eggs

1 Heat oven to 350°F. Spray 9-inch glass pie plate with cooking spray.

2 In medium bowl, stir all ingredients until blended. Pour into pie plate.

3 Bake 35 to 40 minutes or until knife inserted in center comes out clean. Cool 30 minutes.

4 Refrigerate about 2 hours or until chilled. Store covered in refrigerator.

1 Serving Calories 210; Total Fat 5g (Saturated Fat 2.5g, Trans Fat 0g); Cholesterol 65mg; Sodium 180mg; Total Carbohydrate 34g (Dietary Fiber 1g); Protein 6g **Exchanges:** 1½ Starch, 1 Other Carbohydrate, 1 Fat **Carbohydrate Choices:** 2

Kitchen Secret: For a festive presentation, sprinkle the plate with ground cinnamon. Top the pie with whipped topping and a sprinkle of cinnamon.

Kitchen Secret: If you don't have pumpkin pie spice on hand, use our homemade recipe on page 264.

15-minute prep
8 ingredients or less

EXTRA-EASY STREUSEL APPLE PIE

PREP TIME: 15 minutes | **START TO FINISH:** 2 hours 45 minutes | Makes 8 servings

PRESS-IN-THE-PAN CRUST

1½	cups Original Bisquick mix
¼	cup butter, softened
3	tablespoons boiling water

FILLING

1	can (21 oz) apple pie filling

STREUSEL

1	cup Original Bisquick mix
½	cup packed brown sugar
3	tablespoons cold butter

1 Heat oven to 375°F.

2 In medium bowl, mix 1½ cups Original Bisquick mix and ¼ cup softened butter with fork until crumbly. Add boiling water; stir vigorously with fork until dough forms. Gather into ball. Press firmly and evenly against bottom and up side of ungreased 9-inch glass pie plate; flute edge. Spoon Filling evenly into crust.

3 In small bowl, mix Streusel ingredients except butter. Cut in butter, using pastry blender or fork, until crumbly (mixture will look dry). Sprinkle over filling.

4 Bake 15 minutes. Cover top of pie with foil; bake 10 to 15 minutes longer or until golden brown.

5 Cool 2 to 3 hours before serving.

1 Serving Calories 380; Total Fat 13g (Saturated Fat 7g, Trans Fat 0g); Cholesterol 25mg; Sodium 440mg; Total Carbohydrate 61g (Dietary Fiber 1g); Protein 3g **Exchanges:** 1 Starch, 3 Other Carbohydrate, 2½ Fat **Carbohydrate Choices:** 4

Kitchen Secret: If you want to make this for dinner tonight, make the pie first. That way it can be baking and cooling while you prepare and eat dinner. For an extra-special treat, top with Sweetened Whipped Cream (page 276) and serve it drizzled with caramel ice-cream topping—delicious!

* 15-minute prep
* 8 ingredients or less
* 30 minutes or less

SWEETENED WHIPPED CREAM

PREP TIME: 10 minutes | **START TO FINISH:** 15 minutes | Makes 1 to 2 cups

FOR 1 CUP SWEETENED WHIPPED CREAM

- ½ cup heavy whipping cream
- 1 tablespoon powdered or granulated sugar
- ½ teaspoon vanilla

FOR 1½ CUPS SWEETENED WHIPPED CREAM

- ¾ cup heavy whipping cream
- 2 tablespoons powdered or granulated sugar
- 1 teaspoon vanilla

FOR 2 CUPS SWEETENED WHIPPED CREAM

- 1 cup heavy whipping cream
- 2 tablespoons powdered or granulated sugar
- 1 teaspoon vanilla

1 Chill bowl and mixer whisk attachment or regular beaters in freezer or refrigerator 10 to 20 minutes or until cold to the touch (cream whips faster using this technique). For 1 or 1½ Cups Sweetened Whipped Cream, use medium deep bowl; for 2 Cups Sweetened Whipped Cream, use large deep bowl.

2 In chilled bowl, beat all ingredients with electric mixer on low speed until mixture begins to thicken. Gradually increase speed to high and beat just until soft peaks form, lifting whisk or beaters occasionally to check thickness. Do not overbeat or mixture will curdle and begin to form butter. If using whisk attachment, cream will thicken and form soft peaks more quickly.

2 Tablespoons Calories 60; Total Fat 6g (Saturated Fat 3.5g, Trans Fat 0g); Cholesterol 20mg; Sodium 5mg; Total Carbohydrate 1g (Dietary Fiber 0g); Protein 0g **Exchanges:** 1 Fat **Carbohydrate Choices:** 0

METRIC CONVERSION GUIDE

VOLUME

U.S. UNITS	CANADIAN METRIC	AUSTRALIAN METRIC
¼ teaspoon	1 mL	1 ml
½ teaspoon	2 mL	2 ml
1 teaspoon	5 mL	5 ml
1 tablespoon	15 mL	20 ml
¼ cup	50 mL	60 ml
⅓ cup	75 mL	80 ml
½ cup	125 mL	125 ml
⅔ cup	150 mL	170 ml
¾ cup	175 mL	190 ml
1 cup	250 mL	250 ml
1 quart	1 liter	1 liter
1½ quarts	1.5 liters	1.5 liters
2 quarts	2 liters	2 liters
2½ quarts	2.5 liters	2.5 liters
3 quarts	3 liters	3 liters
4 quarts	4 liters	4 liters

WEIGHT

U.S. UNITS	CANADIAN METRIC	AUSTRALIAN METRIC
1 ounce	30 grams	30 grams
2 ounces	55 grams	60 grams
3 ounces	85 grams	90 grams
4 ounces (¼ pound)	115 grams	125 grams
8 ounces (½ pound)	225 grams	225 grams
16 ounces (1 pound)	455 grams	500 grams
1 pound	455 grams	0.5 kilogram

NOTE: The recipes in this cookbook have not been developed or tested using metric measures. When converting recipes to metric, some variations in quality may be noted.

MEASUREMENTS

INCHES	CENTIMETERS
1	2.5
2	5.0
3	7.5
4	10.0
5	12.5
6	15.0
7	17.5
8	20.5
9	23.0
10	25.5
11	28.0
12	30.5
13	33.0

TEMPERATURES

FAHRENHEIT	CELSIUS
32°	0°
212°	100°
250°	120°
275°	140°
300°	150°
325°	160°
350°	180°
375°	190°
400°	200°
425°	220°
450°	230°
475°	240°
500°	260°

INDEX

Note: Page references in *italics* indicate photographs.